westermann

W0186034

fit fürs abi EXPRESS

Englisch

fit fürs abi EXPRESS

Englisch

Autorin:
Sarah Nowonty stammt aus London und verfügt über langjährige Erfahrung als Englischlehrerin. Außerdem arbeitet sie als freie Autorin und Übersetzerin.

westermann GRUPPE

Druck A[1] / Jahr 2019
Alle Drucke der Serie A sind im Unterricht parallel verwendbar.

Redaktion: imprint, Zusmarshausen
Kontakt: finale@westermanngruppe.de
Layout und Umschlaggestaltung: tiff.any, Berlin
Umschlagfoto: iStockphoto.com, Nikada
Druck und Bindung: westermann druck GmbH, Braunschweig

ISBN 978-3-7426-**0113**-1

SO FUNKTIONIERT'S

Fit fürs Abi Express Englisch hilft Ihnen, alle prüfungsrelevanten Themen schnell und effektiv zu wiederholen. Sie finden hier einen **kompakten Überblick** des gesamten Abiturstoffs, mit dem Sie Ihre Wissenslücken rasch schließen können.

Schlagen Sie einfach diejenigen Themenbereiche nach, in denen Sie sich noch nicht ganz sattelfest fühlen. Es ist nicht nötig, das Buch von vorne nach hinten durchzuarbeiten. Jedes Kapitel steht für sich und behandelt einen anderen Fachbereich der Prüfung.

Die Abi-Prüfungen unterscheiden sich nach wie vor geringfügig von Bundesland zu Bundesland. Dies gilt vor allem für die mündliche Prüfung. Informieren Sie sich daher bei Ihrer Lehrkraft über die konkret für Sie geltenden Regelungen.

Das Buch enthält zahlreiche **Merkkästen** und **Abi-Tipps**, die Ihnen das Lösen der Prüfungsaufgaben erleichtern. Mithilfe der **Checklisten** am Ende jedes Kapitels können Sie Ihren eigenen Kenntnisstand überprüfen. Vor allem die im Text **fett gedruckten Begriffe** sollen Sie an die wichtigsten Schlagworte erinnern – gehen Sie sicher, dass Sie diese verstanden haben und gegebenenfalls auch ausführlicher erklären können. Dies ist insbesondere für eine mündliche Prüfung sehr wichtig.

Passend zum Buch gibt es eine **App mit interaktiven Multiple-Choice-Aufgaben**. Mit dieser App können Sie alle wichtigen Themen aus dem Buch aktiv und in motivierender Form trainieren. Sie erhalten die kostenlose App auf www.westermann.de/fit-fuers-abi-express.

Viel Erfolg für die Prüfung wünscht Ihnen
Sarah Nowonty

INHALTSVERZEICHNIS

SO FUNKTIONIERT'S — 3

1 DIE PRÜFUNGEN
Die drei Anforderungsbereiche — 6
Mündliche Prüfungen — 10
Methodenkompetenzen für die schriftliche Prüfung — 12

2 MITSCHRIFTEN UND NOTIZEN — 16

3 GRAMMAR
Use of the tenses — 21
The passive voice — 26
Conditional sentences — 27
Use of the gerund — 29
Phrasal verbs — 31

4 TALKING POINTS: BRITAIN
Politics in Britain — 32
The role of the monarchy — 36
British society — 39
Britain and the world — 46
Britain and Europe — 55

5 TALKING POINTS: USA
Politics in the USA — 58
Religion in the USA — 63
America: the land of opportunity — 68
The Civil Rights Movement — 74
Crime and punishment in the US — 78

6 TALKING POINTS: GLOBALISATION
What is globalisation? — 83
Globalisation and the economy — 84
Globalisation and the environment — 89
Global organisations — 96
Global communication: the role of the internet — 97

7 TALKING POINTS: SCIENCE AND ETHICS
Genetic engineering — 102

DIE SPRACHLICHE LEISTUNG IM ABITUR — 83 **8**

DIE INTERPRETATION LITERARISCHER TEXTE **9**

Lyrik *(poetry)* — 111
Dramatik *(drama)* — 118
Erzählende Literatur/Epik *(narration)* — 124

ANALYSE UND INTERPRETATION VON SACHTEXTEN **10**

Sachtext-Typen — 129
Sachtexte – der Inhalt — 131
Analyse eines Sachtextes — 132

ANALYSE UND INTERPRETATION VON VISUELLEN MATERIALIEN **11**

Ein Bild beschreiben — 136
Ein Bild interpretieren — 138
Eine Karikatur analysieren — 139
Filme analysieren — 141

KRITERIEN DER ZIELTEXTFORMATE **12**

Brief *(letter)* — 143
E-Mail — 144
Rede *(speech)* — 145
Berichte und Artikel *(reports and newspaper articles)* — 146
Literarische Texte *(literary texts)* — 148
Eine *composition* schreiben — 149

LITERATUR-GESCHICHTE IM ÜBERBLICK **13**

Renaissance & 16. Jahrhundert — 152
Das 17. Jahrhundert — 153
Das 18. Jahrhundert — 154
Das 19. Jahrhundert — 155
Das 20. Jahrhundert — 156

STICHWORTVERZEICHNIS — 158

1 DIE PRÜFUNGEN

Die drei Anforderungsbereiche

DIE PRÜFUNGSKOMPETENZEN

Anforderungsbereich I = Leseverständnis, Textreproduktion
Anforderungsbereich II = Auseinandersetzung mit einem Thema – auf einem Text basierend; möglicherweise Mediation
Anforderungsbereich III = Verarbeitung komplexer Sachverhalte, die Sie im Detail analysieren müssen

Abi Tipp

STRESS LASS NACH!

Vermutlich gibt es keine stressfreie Prüfung. Und das ist auch gut so. – Echt jetzt? werden Sie vielleicht fragen. Ja lautet dann die Antwort. So lange die Lücke zwischen dem, was man erreichen will, und dem, was man kann, nicht zu groß ist, nutzt ein gewisser Stresslevel. Die Psychologie spricht dann von Eustress (= positiver Stress). Und dieser positive Stress fördert die Leistungsfähigkeit. Negativer Stress resultiert unter anderem aus dem Gefühl, überfordert zu sein.
Wie kann man das vermeiden? Erstens hilft es zu wissen, was einen bei Prüfungen erwartet. Dazu soll dieses erste Kapitel dienen.
Und zweitens: Jede Art der Vorbereitungsarbeit reduziert die Gefahr, tatsächlich in eine Situation der Überforderung zu kommen. Die weiteren Kapitel des Buches helfen Ihnen bei der Vorbereitung. Und das sogar, wenn Sie möglicherweise denken, nicht mehr genügend Zeit zu haben. Legen Sie einfach los, und Sie werden merken, dass Sie hier in Kürze das Wichtigste zusammengefasst vorfinden. So frischen Sie auf, was Sie eigentlich „wissen", und Sie lernen Fakten, Begrifflichkeiten und Vorgehensweisen da, wo möglicherweise tatsächlich noch eine Lücke vorhanden war.

Anforderungsbereich I

- Die Aufgaben basieren auf einem Thema, das Sie im Unterricht schon behandelt haben.
- Sie zeigen, dass Sie einen Text zu diesem Thema verstehen und bearbeiten können.
- Sie lösen Aufgaben zu einem Text oder einer Abbildung mit eigenen Worten.
- Eine der Aufgaben kann auch eine Mediation sein, bei der Sie die Antwort auf Deutsch formulieren.

Typische Aufgabestellung	Beispiel
complete	*Complete the sentence with words from the text.*
describe = give detailed information	*Describe the woman in the centre of the photo.*
fill in/fill the gaps	*Fill in the gaps with words from the box.*
match	*Match each heading to the correct paragraph.*
outline = state the main points	*Outline the author's opinion of Britain's role in the European Union.*
point out = find and explain certain aspects	*Point out the ways in which the author shows her disapproval of ...*
present = reproduce in your own words; quote from the text to support your answer	*Present the main difficulty facing the characters.*
state = explain clearly	*State the main problems facing the two characters.*
summarise/write a summary	*Summarise the arguments made in favour of immigration.*
tick = put a tick (✓) next to the correct answer	*Which adjectives best describe the mood during the family meal?*

Anforderungsbereich II

- Sie gehen vertieft auf ein Thema ein, das in einem vorgelegten Text behandelt wird.
- Es ist möglich, dass Sie hier eine umfangreichere Mediationsaufgabe bearbeiten müssen.

- Es wird erwartet, dass Sie Kenntnisse aus dem Unterricht einbringen, die über die Textvorlage hinausgehen, die aber einen Bezug auf das allgemeine Thema haben.

Typische Aufgabestellung	**Beispiel**
analyse = separate the task into different parts and examine them in detail; draw a conclusion	*Analyse the use of metaphor in this passage.*
characterise = describe a person's character; give examples	*Characterise Tom's sister and her role in his story.*
compare/contrast = find similarities and differences; give examples	*Compare Jamila's experience with that of other second-generation immigrants in Britain.*
contrast/juxtapose = describe and analyse the differences between two or more things	*Contrast the attitudes of the two speakers towards global warming.*
delineate = present the central elements of an action or argument	*Delineate the problem of the "brain drain".*
describe = paint a detailed picture in words	*Describe Romeo's reaction to meeting Juliet.*
examine = describe and explain certain aspects in detail	*Examine the narrative perspective and its effect on the reader.*
explain = describe in detail; give reasons	*Explain the symbolic meaning of sleep in "Macbeth".*
illustrate/show = use examples to explain	*Illustrate the protagonist's honesty.*
outline = demonstrate the main features; ignore unimportant details	*Outline the author's opinion of Britain's role in the European Union.*
point out = find and explain certain aspects	*Point out the author's attitude towards ...*
put into the context of = link a statement or argument to a relevant historical or current event (based on facts learned in class)	*Put this report into the context of Britain's relationship with the European Union.*
relate = take one aspect of a text and demonstrate its connection to e.g. a text you have studied in class, showing the relationship between them	*Relate this cartoon to the immigrant experience in Britain.*
summarise/sum up = give a brief overview of the main points in your own words	*Summarise the author's main arguments in this extract.*

Anforderungsbereich III

- Es gibt im Regelfall eine größere Auswahl von Aufgabenstellungen: Sie bearbeiten eine davon.
- In diesem Bereich können es Aufgaben zum literarischen Schwerpunktthema oder zu landeskundlichen Themen sein, auch eine Verknüpfung von beidem ist denkbar.
- Sie zeigen, dass Sie komplexe Sachverhalte bearbeiten können.
- Sie müssen Ihre Meinung begründet äußern.
- Sie verwenden dabei Kenntnisse und Arbeitstechniken, die Sie im Unterricht erworben haben.

Typische Aufgabestellung	Beispiel
assess/evaluate = present advantages and disadvantages and form an opinion	*Assess whether the author gets his message across effectively.*
comment on/state = clearly demonstrate your opinion; give specific examples to support this	*Comment on the relevance of the "American Dream" in the USA today.*
contrast = explain the differences between two points	*Contrast this depiction of immigration with other accounts you have studied.*
discuss = analyse all aspects of an issue; make arguments for and against it; support your conclusion with relevant arguments	*Discuss the pros and cons of genetic engineering.*
interpret = determine the meaning of the text in its wider context; discuss the author's message; explain the purpose of a particular aspect of the text	*Interpret the message of the cartoon.*
justify = show reasons for decisions or conclusions	*Justify the protagonist's attitude towards his father.*
write a ... = write a text in a certain style	*Write a reply to the e-mail from the protagonist's sister.*

Mündliche Prüfungen

VERSCHIEDENE ARTEN DER PRÜFUNG

Informieren Sie sich, welche Art der Prüfung für Ihr Bundesland vorgesehen ist. Grundsätzlich gibt es zwei Formen:
Präsentationsprüfung = Referat + Fachgespräch
Kolloquium = Kurzreferat + Gespräch

Wichtig ist auf jeden Fall das Gespräch mit Ihrer Lehrkraft über die Ausgestaltung der Prüfung an Ihrer Schule.

Präsentationsprüfung

- Sie bereiten die Präsentation vor.
- Danach führen Sie ein Fachgespräch mit dem Prüfer: Sie besprechen die Inhalte Ihres Referats und andere Themen.
- In manchen Bundesländern müssen Sie eine schriftliche Übersicht zu Ihrer Präsentation (inklusive Inhalt, Ablauf und verwendete Quellen) eine Woche nach Erhalt der Aufgabenstellung abgeben.

Bei der Präsentation sollten Sie Folgendes beachten:

- selbstsichere Körpersprache
- Blickkontakt mit den Zuhörern herstellen
- deutlich sprechen
- die zur Verfügung stehende Zeit einhalten
- aktiv auf Fragen reagieren
- angemessener Einsatz von Medien
- möglichst Informationen aus verschiedenen Quellen
- Struktur: Die Präsentation braucht jeweils klar erkennbar eine Einleitung, einen Hauptteil und einen Abschluss.
- Zusammenhänge verdeutlichen
- Schwerpunkte setzen
- Argumente gut begründen

Im Gespräch im Anschluss an die Präsentation ist Folgendes wichtig:

- Nehmen Sie aktiv daran teil.
- Verteidigen Sie Ihre Argumente sachlich, begründen Sie.
- Verwenden Sie gelernte Formulierungen – etwa zum Zustimmen, um Gegenargument zu bringen ...).
- Antworten Sie ausführlich – nicht nur mit „ja“ oder „nein“.
- Auch im Gespräch ist Ihre Körpersprache wichtig (nicken, lächeln, Augenkontakt).

Abi Tipp

ZEIT GUT EINTEILEN!

Wenn Sie Ihre Präsentation üben, stoppen Sie, wie lange Sie dafür brauchen. Sind Sie zu schnell, wirkt es zu gehetzt. Sind Sie aber zu langsam, könnte Ihnen die Zeit ausgehen, was auch keinen guten Eindruck macht.

Kolloquium

- Sie bekommen ca. 30 Minuten vor Prüfungsbeginn das Thema, über das Sie ein Kurzreferat halten müssen.
- Möglicherweise bekommen Sie auch Materialien, die bei der Vorbereitung helfen.
- Die Vorbereitung auf das Referat erfolgt unter Aufsicht.
- In der Prüfung halten Sie Ihre Präsentation; danach folgt ein Gespräch über diese und andere Themen.
- Auch hier achten Sie bitte auf alle oben erwähnten Hinweise zu Körperhaltung etc.

Methodenkompetenzen für die schriftliche Prüfung

PRÜFUNGSTECHNIKEN

In der Prüfung haben Sie nur begrenzt Zeit, sich mit einem Text auseinanderzusetzen und diesen zu bearbeiten. Deshalb müssen Sie die erlernten Techniken gekonnt einsetzen:

- Lesetechniken = Worum geht es?
- Worterschließungstechniken = Wie verstehe ich unbekannte Worte?
- Umgang mit dem Wörterbuch = Wie verwende ich es schnell und effektiv?

Erster Schritt: Welche Art Text liegt vor?

Textgattung identifizieren

Handelt es sich um einen

- Sachtext *(non-fictional text)*
- → Essay, Zeitungsartikel, Brief, Rede ...?
- fiktionalen Text *(fictional text)*
- → Erzählung, Drama, Gedicht?

Gibt es Angaben

- zu Autor/Autorin,
- zum Titel des Textes,
- zum Erscheinungsdatum?

Falls der Text von einer Abbildung begleitet wird:

- Wie ist das Verhältnis von Text und Abbildung?
- → Bietet die Abbildung zusätzliche Informationen?
- → Ist sie lediglich eine optisch attraktive Beigabe?
- Die häufigsten Abbildungstypen sind:
- → Ein Objekt, ein Handlungselement aus dem Text wird dargestellt.
- → Informationen aus dem Text werden als Schaubild umgesetzt.
- → Komplexere Sachverhalte werden graphisch und modellhaft abgebildet.

Lesetechniken – die nötige Infos finden

Lesetechniken

Skimming

- Der Text wird schnell überflogen, um das Wichtigste zu entdecken.

Nützlich für Aufgabestellungen wie:

→ *Point out the main issues dealt with in the article.*

→ *What is the essay about?*

Scanning

- Wenn Sie spezifische Informationen aus einem Text brauchen, z. B. um gut zu argumentieren, suchen Sie beim Lesen zunächst nach den *key words*, die Sie brauchen. Die Abschnitte, in denen die *key words* erscheinen, lesen Sie dann intensiv durch.

Nützlich für Aufgabestellungen wie:

→ *Illustrate the author's attitude towards climate change.*

Intensive reading

- Hier wird der Text sehr gründlich gelesen. Sie analysieren alles von Aufbau und Struktur bis zu den genutzten Stilmitteln. Markieren Sie wichtige Stellen und machen Sie am Rand Notizen.

Nützlich für Aufgabestellungen wie:

→ *Describe the effect of the narrative perspective and stylistic devices in this passage.*

Worterschließungstechniken

Wenn Ihnen ein unbekanntes Wort begegnet, müssen Sie nicht sofort zum Wörterbuch greifen. Es ist oft möglich, ein Wort zu erschließen:

- ***Intelligent guessing* im Textzusammenhang =** Der Kontext macht oft deutlich, was das Wort bedeutet.
- ***Intelligent guessing* durch die Wortfamilie =** Ihre Kenntnisse über Wortbildung helfen Ihnen, die Bedeutung des Wortes herauszufinden. Hier sind gerade Vor- und Nachsilben hilfreich.

Vorsilbe und Bedeutung	Beispiele
bi- = zwei	*bicycle, biceps, binary, biweekly, biathlon*
co-, con-, com- = begleitend, zusammen mit	*co-author, compact, combine, convert, contract*

Vorsilbe und Bedeutung	Beispiele
contra-, counter- = gegen, Gegenteil	*contradict, contrary, contrast, counterargument, counterpoint*
de-, dis-, dif- = loswerden, nicht, Gegenteil von	*demotivate, demoralise, dismiss, disagree, differ, disrespect*
in-, im-, il-, ir- = nicht	*illegal, immortal, impossible, inaccurate, insecure, irregular*
mis- = falsch, irregeleitet	*mistake, misinterpret, mispronounce, mislead*
out- = besser, höher, darüber hinaus	*outnumber, outdo, outperform, outburst,*
over- = zu viel, darüber hinweg	*overeat, overdo, overcome, overlap, overlook*
post- = nach, später	*postpone, postwar, postgraduate*
pre- = voher, davor	*prebook, preview, preorder, prepare, preliminary*
re- = wieder, zurück	*return, retract, revise, rename, recalculate, reply*
semi- = halb	*semifinal, semiconscious, semicircle, semi-detached*
sub- = unter	*submerge, submarine, subconscious, substandard*

Abi Tipp

WORTFAMILIEN AUFSCHREIBEN!

Wenn Sie ein neues Wort notieren, ist es hilfreich, auch andere grammatikalische Formen des Wortes aufzuschreiben.

Beispiel: *to employ; employment; unemployment; employee* etc.

Sie erweitern dadurch Ihren Wortschatz und bekommen ein besseres Gefühl dafür, wie Grammatik funktioniert.

Sie können natürlich zudem Ihre Kenntnisse anderer Sprachen verwenden, um durch ***intelligent guessing* mithilfe der Sprachgeschichte** Wörter zu erschließen. Viele englische Wörter haben germanische, französische, lateinische oder altgriechische Wurzeln und ähneln deshalb Wörtern, die Sie kennen.

Wörterbücher verwenden

Wenn Sie ein Wort in einem zweisprachiges Wörterbuch nachschlagen, sollen Sie nicht einfach den ersten Begriff nehmen, ohne zu kontrollieren, ob dies wirklich das Wort ist, das Sie brauchen. Lesen Sie alle Angaben, bevor Sie ein Wort auswählen. Es ist hilfreich, das ausgewählte Wort zusätzlich in einem einsprachigen Wörterbuch nachzuschlagen, um mehr zu dessen Bedeutung und Verwendung zu erfahren.

Was ein Wörterbuch noch alles kann

- Es gibt die Wortart an (Substantiv, Verb, Adjektiv, usw.).
- Der Sprachgebrauch wird abgebildet: Es wird beispielsweise geklärt, ob das Verb mit *to infinitive* oder *-ing* verwendet wird.
- Es listet die anderen Formen des Wortes auf.
- Es gibt die Aussprache in phonetischer Schrift an.
- Es gibt Beispiele von Kollokationen an: Mit welchen anderen Wörtern wird es verwendet? z. B. *to be interested* ***in*** *something*

DIE PRÜFUNGEN — **Checkliste**

- → Informieren Sie sich über den genauen Ablauf und die Inhalte der Prüfungen in Ihrem Bundesstaat.
- → Vergewisserns Sie sich, dass Sie die Unterschiede zwischen den verschiedenen Aufgabestellungen verstehen.
- → Was müssen Sie bei der mündlichen Prüfung beachten?
- → Welche Lesetechnik können Sie verwenden, um einen Überblick über den Text zu bekommen?
- → Welche Lesetechnik ist geeignet, bestimmte Informationen zu identifizieren?
- → Warum ist es hilfreich, die Bedeutung von Vor- und Nachsilben zu wissen?
- → Wie kann man die Bedeutung eines unbekannten Wortes auch ohne Wörterbuch herausfinden?
- → Warum ist es hilfreich, auch mit einsprachigen und nicht nur mit zweisprachigen Wörterbücher zu arbeiten?

2 MITSCHRIFTEN UND NOTIZEN

Mitschreiben ist ein wichtiger Teil des Schulalltags. Wenn Sie während des Unterrichts klare, übersichtliche Notizen machen, haben Sie eine gute Basis sowohl für Hausarbeiten als auch für die Prüfungszeit, wenn Sie den Unterrichtsstoff wiederholen müssen.

NOTIZEN MACHEN: METHODEN

Es gibt viele verschiedene Mitschreibtechniken. Natürlich muss jeder für sich entscheiden, welche Technik für ihn/sie am effektivsten ist. Beim Mitschreiben in der Schule ist es auf jeden Fall hilfreich, Folgendes anzuwenden/zu beherzigen:

- Stichworte
- Abkürzungen, Kürzel und Symbole
- kurze Absätze
- klare Überschriften, die den Inhalt zusammenfassen
- nummerierte Seiten
- Ränder für zusätzliche Notizen freilassen
- verschiedene Farben
- die Notizen in verschiedene Ordner für die unterschiedlichen Fächer abheften

Technik	Beispiele
Stichworte	Verwendung von Listen und Aufzählungspunkte (*bullets*)
Abkürzungen und Kürzel	Entwickeln Sie Ihre eigene Kürzel für häufig vorkommende Begriffe; für Namen schreiben Sie nach der ersten Erwähnung nur die Initialen auf.
Symbole	Pfeile, Kästchen, Punkte, Linien: Die Zusammenhänge zwischen verschiedene Informationen können auf einen Blick erfasst werden.
kurze Absätze mit klaren Überschriften	Notizen werden/bleiben dadurch übersichtlich.
nummerierte Seiten	Unabdingbar, wenn Sie auf lose Blätter schreiben, die später in einem Ordner ablegt werden.

Technik	Beispiele
Ränder freilassen	Besonders praktisch, wenn Sie Ihre Notizen später durchlesen: So sind die Notizen einfach zu ergänzen oder auszubessern, ohne dass sie unübersichtlich werden.
verschiedene Farben	Viele Menschen finden es einfacher, mit Notizen zu arbeiten, die ein visuelles Element haben. Mit verschiedene Stiftfarben können Sie zwischen diversen Aspekten unterscheiden.
in verschiedene Ordner abheften	So müssen Sie nicht Stapel loser Papiere durchwühlen, bis Sie die Notizen zu einem bestimmten Thema finden.

Abi Tipp

NOTIZEN ALS LERNBASIS

Oft werden Sie zu einem späteren Zeitpunkt Ihre Notizen verwenden müssen, um für eine Prüfung zu lernen. Deswegen ist es wichtig, diese von Anfang an klar zu strukturieren. Wenn dies für Sie während des Unterrichts schwierig ist (weil Sie etwa nicht so gut gleichzeitig zuhören und mitschreiben können), ist es umso wichtiger, die Notizen so bald wie möglich noch einmal durchzugehen und zu kontrollieren, solange Sie den Stoff noch frisch im Kopf haben. Dadurch sichern Sie, dass Sie vor der Prüfung wirklich noch etwas mit den Notizen anfangen können.

Von Zeit zu Zeit müssen Sie bestimmte Themen eigenständig recherchieren: für ein Referat, ein Essay, die Facharbeit oder als Vorbereitung für eine mündliche Prüfung. Dazu stehen Ihnen heutzutage viel mehr Ressourcen als nur die Bibliothek zur Verfügung:

- Webseiten,
- Lernvideos,
- Apps.

Die Techniken, mit denen Sie relevante Informationen in einem Buch identifizieren, können Sie natürlich auch für Online-Artikel usw. verwenden:

Lesetechniken

- **Skimming =** Beim Durchlesen des Textes versuchen Sie, dem Text die wesentlichen Informationen zu entnehmen. Es geht um einen Überblick.
- **Scanning =** Beim Scanning suchen Sie gezielt nach Textstellen, die für die Beantwortung von konkreten Fragen wichtig sind, das sind beispielsweise bestimmte Schlüsselstellen, Namen oder Jahreszahlen.
- **Intensive reading =** Der Text wird intensiv gelesen und bearbeitet.
  Verwenden Sie beispielswese verschiedene Farben, um relevante Informationen zu markieren. Machen Sie am Rand Notizen. Sie können dabei Symbole, wie sie auf Seite 16 erwähnt sind, verwenden, um alles übersichtlich zu halten. Sollte der Text nicht mit einem Zeilenzähler versehen sein, kann es nützlich sein, selbst einen neben den Text zu schreiben. Eine Durchnummerierung von Absätzen ist bei einem längeren Text ebenfalls zu empfehlen.

Einen Aufsatz/ein Referat planen

Es gibt verschiedene Methoden, Informationen für einen geplanten Aufsatz oder Referat zu organisieren:

Wenn Sie vergleichend schreiben sollen, können Sie **Tabellen *(tables)*** oder **Raster *(grids)*** verwenden.
Beispiel: *Compare the problems the characters in the two stories face as second-generation immigrants in Britain.*

Story 1	Story 2
The protagonist respects her family and their values.	The protagonist rebels against her parents.
She is prepared to marry the husband her parents have chosen for her, even though she doesn't love him.	She leads a double life: her life in the home and outside it.
...	...

Um eine Abfolge zu beschreiben oder eine Zusammenfassung zu erstellen, ist ein **Flussdiagramm (*flow chart*)** hilfreich:
Beispiel: *Outline the main events in each act of* Macbeth.

ACT 1 ← There has been a battle that Macbeth has helped to win. He meets three witches who tell him he will be king. The ambitious Lady Macbeth plans to kill King Duncan when he visits their home. Macbeth is persuaded to go along with her plan.

↓

ACT 2

↓

ACT 3

↓

ACT 4

↓

ACT 5

Wenn Sie Ideen für eine Erörterung sammeln müssen, ist **Brainstorming** eine Methode, viele Ideen zu einem Thema zu sammeln.

Der nächste notwendige Schritt ist die Auswahl und das logische Ordnen der Argumente.

Beispiel: *What is the "American Dream" and how did it shape America? Do you think it is still relevant today?*

Definition of the American Dream	▪ ▪
Ways that it shaped America	▪ ▪
Relevance today	▪ ▪
Conclusion with my personal opinion	▪ ▪

Eine weitere Methode, Ideen für eine Erörterung zu sammeln, ist das **Baumdiagramm *(mind map)***. Da schreiben Sie den zentralen Begriff in die Mitte und entwickeln von dort aus ein Netzwerk von Ideen.
Beispiel: *What are the advantages and disadvantages of a multi-cultural society?*

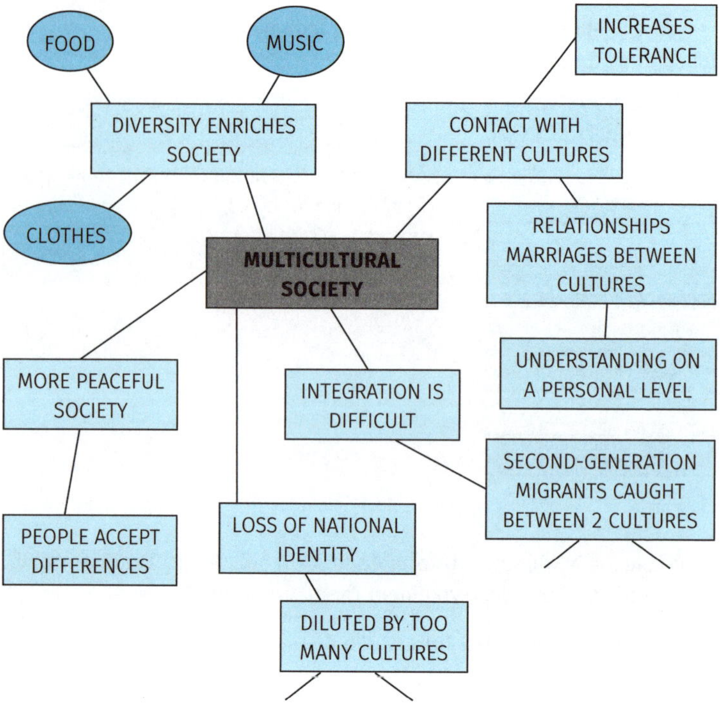

MITSCHRIFTEN UND NOTIZEN — Checkliste

- Gut organisierte Notizen sind das A und O.
- Verwenden Sie Techniken, mit denen Sie Notizen schnell aber übersichtlich erfassen können.
- Visuelle Aspekte der Notizen, z. B. Farben, ermöglichen einen besseren Überblick.
- Verwenden Sie Lesetechniken wie *skimming* oder *scanning*, um die von Ihnen benötigten Informationen schneller zu finden.
- Planen Sie Ihre Aufsätze, indem Sie Ihre Ideen aufschreiben und gut strukturieren, bevor Sie zum Schreiben anfangen.

GRAMMAR

Use of the tenses

Simple and progressive forms

For a quick overview of how to use the simple and progressive forms in English, see the examples below:

Use of the simple present	Examples
things that are generally true:	Many people **drink** coffee.
natural facts and scientific laws:	Cats **have** four legs.
regular, repeated actions; routines:	Tom usually **cycles** to work.
permanent situations:	Berlin **is** the capital of Germany.
state verbs (generally only used in the simple form)	This soup **tastes** delicious!
after time clauses (*when, if, until, as soon as, etc*)	Emma will be surprised when she **hears** our news!

Abi Tipp

GOOD TO KNOW:

Signal words for the simple present:

- always, usually, often, sometimes, occasionally, never, every
- if, when, until, as soon as
- to be, to believe, to belong, to consist, to contain, to depend, to hate, to know, to like, to love, to mean, to need, to prefer, to realise, to remember, to seem, to smell, to taste, to want

Use of the present progressive	Examples
actions happening at the moment of speaking:	It'**s raining** heavily – you'd better take an umbrella.
incomplete actions:	We'**re learning** about the Cold War in history.
temporary situations:	My cousin **is staying** with us for a few days.
changing or developing situations:	The effects of global warming **are getting** worse.

The past tenses work in a similar way:

Use of the simple past	Examples
permanent or long-lasting situations in the past:	His family **owned** the land for many generations.
repeated actions and routines:	The film club **met** every Monday afternoon in the cinema.
completed actions:	The factory **closed** down in 2015.
actions in a sequence:	She **pressed** the button, the door **opened** and she **stepped** into the lift.
state verbs	This painting **belonged** to my grandmother.

Use of the past progressive	Examples
temporary situations in the past:	I stayed at home last night because I **wasn't feeling** well.
activities happening at a definite time in the past:	Three weeks ago we **were skiing** in Austria.
actions not complete at a certain time in the past:	They **were talking** about Lucy when she came into the room.

Abi Tipp

GOOD TO KNOW:

We often use the simple past and past progressive to show that one action interrupted another:

- We **were having** a barbecue when it **started** to rain.
- I **saw** Tina while I **was waiting** for the bus.

The perfect tenses

Perfect tenses are used in a number of different situations in English:

Use of the present perfect simple	Examples
recent events, without saying exactly when they took place:	Tom **has** just **left**. He'll be back this afternoon.
results of past actions that have an effect on the present:	If you **haven't revised** for this test, you're likely to fail it.
for things someone has experienced at some time in their life; exactly when is not mentioned:	She**'s visited** New York several times.

Use of the present perfect simple	Examples
situations that began in the past and have continued to the present:	They'**ve lived** in that house for over 20 years.
for routines or repeated actions that began in the past and have continued until the present:	I'**ve** never **missed** an episode of "Lost Kingdoms" – I watch it every week!
for time expressions that indicate unfinished time:	There **hasn't been** much snow so far this winter.
for state verbs:	We'**ve known** each other since we were children.

Contrast of the present perfect simple and the present perfect progressive

In some cases, there is no real difference in meaning between the simple and progressive forms of the present perfect:

- I'**ve worked** here for several years *or* I'**ve been working** here for several years.

However, the focus of the sentence is different, depending on whether the simple or progressive form is used:

→ The present perfect progressive focuses on the activity, whereas the simple form focuses on the result:

- I'**ve been revising** for the maths test all week.
- I'**ve** just **found out** that I'**ve passed** the test – what a relief!

→ The progressive form shows that an action is not complete, whereas the simple form is used for completed activities:

- They'**ve been renovating** our school this year. The work should be finished by June.
- The building looks much better now they'**ve renovated** it.

→ The progressive form shows how long something has been going on, while the simple form expresses how often something has happened:

- You'**ve been sitting** at your computer all afternoon. Go out and get some fresh air!
- I'**ve** already **walked** the dog twice today – now it's your turn!

→ As with other tenses, the progressive form can be used to show that a situation is temporary, while the simple form indicates a permanent or long-lasting situation:

- I'**ve been looking** everywhere for my phone – I really need to check my messages.
- It seems that I'**ve lost** my phone. I can't find it anywhere.

The present perfect and the simple past

It can be tricky to decide whether you need the present perfect or the simple past. Here are some pointers:

- When you use a specific past time expression (e.g. **yesterday, last week, ago**), you need the simple past:
- *She'**s worked** with many Hollywood legends, most recently with Tom Cruise, whose new film she **directed last year.***
- *"I'**ve** never **been** to the USA. **Have** you?" "No, but I **visited** Canada a couple of years **ago**."*
- Expressions indicating "unfinished" time (e.g. **today, this week**) cannot be used with the present perfect for short, completed actions:
  - *When **did** Tom **leave** this morning?*
  - *(at 10 a.m.): I'**ve sent** a lot of emails this morning.*
  - *(at 5 p.m.): I **sent** a lot of emails this morning.*
- The simple past is used when there is no connection to the present:
  - *Marilyn Monroe starred in several films. (as she is now dead, she will not star in any more films)*
  - *Although she is still young, Jennifer Lawrence **has** already **starred** in several films.*
- The present perfect is often used to introduce new information, followed by the simple past to continue the story:
  - *President Jones **has won** the election. Experts **expected** a close result, but when the votes **were counted**, she **was** the clear winner.*

The past perfect tenses

Use of the past perfect simple	Examples
for past events that happened before other events in the past:	When Lucy **had finished** her essay, she **switched off** the computer.

Use of the past perfect progressive	Examples
for events that happened before another past event, the result of which could still be seen later:	It **had been raining** for days and the water in the river was dangerously high.
for situations that continued for a while up to a certain time in the past:	We were relieved when Ben finally phoned – we **had been waiting** for his call all day.
for talking about how long an activity or event went on:	Jane **had been drinking** coffee all afternoon and couldn't sleep at all that night!

The future forms

Abi Tipp

GOOD TO KNOW:

Remember that there are several different ways to talk about the future in English!

- will/won't — the future progressive
- going to — the present tenses
- the future perfect simple and progressive

Study the examples below to make sure you know which form to use!

Use of will/won't	Examples
for the future in general:	The tickets **will be** more expensive in summer, so we should buy them now.
for making future predictions:	England **won't win** this match – not the way they're playing!
for spontaneous offers, promises or decisions:	If you like, **I'll help** you with your maths homework.

Use of the future progressive	Examples
for activities not yet complete at a particular time in the future:	Come round at 8 o'clock – **I'll be waiting** for you.
for things that are definitely going to happen at a certain time in the future:	The next Olympic Games **will be taking place** in Tokyo in 2020.

Use of the present tenses with a future meaning	Examples
use the present progressive for future arrangements:	We'**re meeting** in the café on Grafton Street.
use the simple present to talk about timetables and schedules:	The concert **begins** at 8 o'clock.

Use of the "going to" future	Examples
for plans or intentions:	I'**m going to save** up my money and buy a new car this year.
for predictions about the future based on evidence in the present:	It'**s going to rain** later: look at those black clouds!

Use of the future perfect simple + progressive	Examples
for actions that will be complete by a certain time in the future:	By the end of June, my brother **will have run** his seventh marathon. I can't believe we'**ll have been living** in Spain for 10 years by the end of April!

The passive voice

HOW TO FORM THE PASSIVE

The passive voice is formed using the verb **to be** in the relevant tense plus the **past participle**.

- The passive places the focus on the action rather than the person that carries it out.
- If it is necessary to mention the person, **by** is used:

→ *The Mona Lisa was painted* **by** *Leonardo da Vinci.*

The passive voice in different tenses	Examples
present simple:	Breakfast **is included** in the price of the room.
present progressive:	Tickets for the festival **are being sold** on the event website.
past simple:	The stolen jewels **were found** in the thief's car.
past progressive	The thief escaped while he **was being taken** to the police station.
present perfect:	Has Marie **been invited** to the party?
past perfect:	By the end of the month, her song **had been downloaded** more than 50,000 times.
"will" future:	Your personal information **won't be made** public.
"going to" future:	His blog **is going to be published** as a book next month.

The passive voice in different tenses	Examples
future perfect:	If we don't hurry, all the food **will have been eaten** by the time we get there!
modal verbs:	Mobile phones **cannot be taken** into the examination room. Bags **should not be left** unattended at any time. The pictures **must have been posted** straight after the party, but we don't know who took them.

Conditional sentences

HOW TO FORM CONDITIONAL SENTENCES

- Conditional sentences consist of two clauses.
- It does not matter whether the main clause or the subordinate clause comes first.
- They are used to talk about what happens, or could happen, or could have happened.
- They are often referred to as "if clauses", but the two clauses can also be linked by **when, unless, until, even if, as long as**.

The zero conditional

The zero conditional is used for things that always happen. The **present simple** is used in both clauses:

→ When it **is** winter in Britain, it **is** summer in South Africa.

→ If you **click** here, you **can** download the photos.

The first conditional

The first conditional is used for things that are likely to happen. Use **will/won't** in the main clause and the **present** in the subordinate clause:

→ I'**ll go** swimming after work if I **have** time.

→ Unless you **work** harder, you **won't** finish your essay on time.

The second conditional

The second conditional is used for things that are impossible or unlikely. Use **would/wouldn't + present** in the main clause and the **past simple/progressive** in the subordinate clause:

→ My father **would go** crazy if he **found** out what really happened last weekend!

→ I don't trust Brian. If I **were** you, I **wouldn't give** him my phone number.

Abi Tipp

GOOD TO KNOW:

If I were you is a standard phrase often used to give someone advice or tell them your opinion. Although **I** + **were** sounds wrong, it is correct. In similar phrases, **if I were rich** or if **I was rich** are both correct.

The third conditional

The third conditional is used to talk about past situations that did not happen, although they were possible, or something that should not have happened, but did. Use **would/wouldn't have + past participle** in the main clause and the **past perfect** in the subordinate clause:

→ He **would have become** the new world champion if he **had won** the race.

→ If I **hadn't forgotten** to put petrol in the car, it **wouldn't have broken** down.

Conditional sentences with modal verbs

Modal verbs can also be used in the main clause of a conditional sentence instead of will or would:

→ You **could get** a better job if you **spoke** a foreign language.

→ If they **hadn't repaired** the fence, someone **might have been injured**.

→ **Let** me know if you **can come** to the cinema with us.

Use of the gerund

WHAT IS A GERUND?

- A gerund is a verb that is used as a noun.
- The form is the same as the present participle ("-ing" form).

- A gerund can be the subject or object of a sentence:
  Snowboarding is more popular than ever this winter.
  I enjoy **baking** – I find it very relaxing.
- Gerunds can also have their own object:
  Taking photos in the museum is forbidden.
  Their parents want them to stop **watching** so much television.

Verbs always followed by the gerund

Some common verbs that are always followed by the gerund are: *admit, appreciate, can't help, can't stand, consider, delay, deny, dislike, enjoy, escape, feel like, finish, forgive, give up, imagine, involve, mention, mind, miss, postpone, practise, put off, resent, risk, suggest, understand*

→ Would you mind **closing** the window? It's freezing in here!
→ She considered **studying** medicine, but the course was too expensive.
→ My cousin really enjoys **traveling** – he's going to Argentina soon.

Verbs that can be followed by the gerund

Some common verbs that can be followed by the gerund are: *forget, hate, like, love, prefer, remember, stop, try*

→ When it comes to exercise, I prefer **cycling** to **jogging**.
→ Stop **telling** me what to do! I can make my own decisions.

The meaning of these verbs changes depending on whether they are followed by a gerund or an infinitive:

followed by a gerund	followed by an infinitive
I **remember checking** my messages but I didn't see yours. = *I know that I did it.*	**Remember to check** your messages later. = *Don't forget to do it.*
Why don't you **try working** in the library? It's a lot quieter in there. = *this is a suggestion of something that might work for you*	She **tried to work** in the corner of the café but found she couldn't concentrate. = *she attempted to work but did not succeed*

Gerunds are used after certain preposition combinations.

verb + preposition + gerund:

- I'm **fed up with listening** to her complain about her boyfriend.
- They're **thinking about moving** to the countryside.
- She **apologised for losing** my book and offered to buy me a new one.

adjective + preposition + gerund:

- I'm **interested in learning** how to windsurf.
- My brother is **afraid of flying**.
- We're very **excited about meeting** the president.

Other common prepositions followed by the gerund:

- **In spite of having** a terrible cold, Tony went to the football match.
- **Besides speaking** French and Italian, she knows a bit of Chinese.
- **After winning** an Olympic gold medal, she decided to end her sporting career.
- I can't believe they went on holiday together **without telling** me.

Gerunds as part of compound nouns

- The hotel has two large **swimming** pools.
- Lunch will be served in the **dining** room.
- It's terrible that so many young people today suffer from **eating** disorders.
- Next week we're going on a **shopping** trip to London.
- Tom wants to be a **racing** car driver when he grows up!
- There is a **waiting** room inside the station.

Gerunds in notices and instructions

- No **smoking.**
- Emergency access road: no **parking** here.
- No **talking** while the exam is in progress.

Phrasal verbs

Abi Tipp

LEARNING PHRASAL VERBS

- It is helpful to write phrasal verbs in a sentence to illustrate the meaning, as it is not always possible to guess their meaning.
- You can organise them by verb (e.g. phrasal verbs with "take" or by particle (e.g. phrasal verbs with "off", "on" and so on).

Phrasal verbs with "come"

- The bill **came to** more than £100, but my father paid.
- They **came up with** some good suggestions at the meeting.

Phrasal verbs with "get"

- It helped me **get through** a difficult time in my life.
- Lena was late because she **got off** the bus at the wrong stop.
- Tim and Harry don't **get on**. They argue all the time.

Phrasal verbs with "put"

- **Put** your jacket **on** before you go out.
- Please **put** your toys **away**. Don't just leave them on the floor!

Phrasal verbs with "off"

- **Take off** your shoes before you go into the living room.
- Jack **fell off** a ladder and broke his arm.

Phrasal verbs with "up"

- Frank walks so fast I can't **keep up** with him.
- I hate having to **get up** so early every day – I'd rather stay in bed.

GRAMMAR Checkliste

Make sure you know:

→ When to use the simple form and when to use the progressive form
→ When to use the simple past and the present perfect
→ The difference between the various future forms
→ How to form the passive
→ How to use conditional sentences
→ When you need the gerund

4

TALKING POINTS: BRITAIN

Politics in Britain

Parliament

The British Parliament is made up of two chambers:

The House of Commons

- The 650 Members of Parliament (MPs), elected by the citizens of Britain, debate current issues, discuss policy and make laws.
- After the last general election (2017), there were 650 MPs, each representing a constituency.
- 32 % of them are women, showing a slight increase in the number of women MPs.
- Strict seating plan: the Prime Minister and the Cabinet sit on the front bench, facing the Leader of the Opposition and the Shadow Cabinet across a table. The other MPs sit behind them and are known as "back-benchers".

The House of Lords

- Traditionally, members were not elected but had an automatic right to a seat there: as an aristocrat, high-ranking member of the Church of England or a life peer (former politicians).
- Following a reform in 1999, most members are now life peers, i.e. people with political experience.
- The Lords have limited powers to influence the political decisions made in the House of Commons. They can suggest changes to laws and delay the passing of a new law for twelve months.
- The House of Lords used to be the highest court of appeal in Britain. However, since 2009, Britain has had a Supreme Court which has taken over these duties.

THE BRITISH ELECTORAL SYSTEM IN BRIEF

→ **General elections:** held every four to five years
→ **The Prime Minister:** can call an election when it best suits their party
→ **Voting system:** "first-past-the-post" → the candidate with the most votes in each constituency wins, even if they have only received a few more votes than the next candidate
→ **Problem:** British politics are dominated by a few large parties → very difficult for small parties to win seats

The political parties

There are two main political parties in the House of Commons and several smaller ones that also have a few seats in London. The smaller, regional parties have seats in the devolved parliaments of Scotland, Wales and Northern Ireland.

Party	Main facts
The Conservative Party	centre-right party; traditionally middle and upper-class voters; known for cuts in public spending, healthcare and social benefits; many supporters of Brexit
The Labour Party	traditionally a left-wing workers' party with close connections to the trade unions
Scottish National Party	centre-left; campaigns for Scottish independence
Green Party	1 MP in London; emphasis on environmental issues
Plaid Cymru	National party of Wales
UK Independence Party (UKIP)	driving force behind the Brexit referendum; accusations of racism
Sinn Féin	main Republican party in Northern Ireland; controversial due to close links with the IRA terrorist group
Democratic Unionist Party	PM Theresa May formed a coalition with this right-wing Northern Irish party in 2017
Brexit Party	Established in 2019. Eurosceptical

Devolution

At the end of the 1990s, separate parliaments were established for Scotland, Wales and Northern Ireland. They do not completely replace the central parliament in London, but have powers to deal with certain political matters on a more regional level.

The Scottish Parliament

- opened in July 1999
- deals with education, health, agriculture, environment, food standards, sport, the arts, transport and tourism
- can pass new laws

The National Assembly for Wales

- opened in 1999
- deals with education, health, economic development and similar issues in Wales

The Northern Ireland Assembly

- established in 1998
- deals with education, health, the environment, the arts
- has been suspended four times due to disagreements between the two main unionist parties (the Democratic Unionist Party and the Ulster Unionist Party, who wish Northern Ireland to remain part of the UK) and the nationalist party Sinn Féin (who would like to see a reunited Ireland).

Scottish independence

Many Scottish people would like to see Scotland leave the United Kingdom and become an independent nation. After many years of political discussion, a referendum on independence was held in September 2014. Several arguments for and against independence were raised at the time:

For independence	Against independence
The citizens of Scotland should be allowed to make their own decisions about the future of their country.	Scotland would have to leave the Schengen area and introduce controls along the Scottish-English border.

For independence	Against independence
Scotland could make its own defence and foreign affairs policies; for example, it could get rid of nuclear weapons in Scottish waters.	Oil is not reliable as a source of income, as production levels are dropping in many parts of the North Sea. Scotland does not have enough other natural resources to make money, and tourism alone would not bring in enough income for a healthy economy.
The country can generate enough income from its natural resources, e.g. North Sea oil, to comfortably exist without the rest of the UK.	Scotland would not be allowed to stay in the EU, losing all the benefits that membership brings. It would have to apply for EU membership, which would take time. Because of this, it would initially have to keep the British pound as its currency.
There would be emphasis on Scottish culture and traditions.	At the time of the referendum, Britain's economy was strong, bringing benefits to Scottish businesses. These businesses would find it harder to win contracts when faced with international competition without the support of the rest of Britain.
Scotland would have greater political influence, e.g. in Europe.	Remaining part of Britain, at that time, meant remaining in the EU, something that is important to the majority of Scottish citizens.

The result of the referendum was that 55 % voted to remain in the UK, while 44 % voted for independence. Two years later, after the Brexit referendum, it became clear that one of the reasons for staying part of the UK, i.e. the right to remain in the EU, no longer applied. Due to this, Scottish National Party and other are now calling for a second referendum on independence before Brexit is made final. However, this seems unlikely to happen within the Brexit timeframe.

The role of the monarchy

Britain is one of the few countries in Europe that is still a monarchy. While some people see the royal family as an integral part of life in Britain, others believe it is time to put an end to what they see as an outdated institution. Instead, they think Britain should become a republic with an elected head of state.

The traditional role of the monarchy

- Until the English Civil War (1642–1651), the monarch was **all-powerful.**
- He/she was the **political head of the country** → could imprison or even execute anyone that disagreed with him/her.
- Starting with Henry VIII (1509–1547), the monarch was also the **head of the Church of England** → additional powers.
- The **English Civil War** was fought between the king and Parliament → dispute over how much control the monarch should have over Parliament.
- The Parliamentarians won and **executed the king**, Charles I.
- The monarchy was restored in 1660 → **the monarch lost the right to control Parliament.**

The monarchy today

The role of the monarch in Britain today is mainly **ceremonial**, although the queen does still play a small political role:

- She is **Head of State** and represents her country at home and abroad.
- She is the official **head of the Church of England**.
- She officially **opens Parliament** each year after the summer recess.
- She **signs bills** before they become law and could even prevent a law from being passed by refusing to sign it. However, this is extremely unlikely to happen.
- She officially **appoints the Prime Minister** after a general election.
- She **meets the Prime Minister** once a week **to discuss current issues** and give advice.
- She **visits her subjects**, often to show support after a disaster.
- The traditional "Queen's Speech" is broadcast every Christmas Day in the afternoon. This speech is a **personal message from the Queen to her subjects** in which she reflects on events of the past year.

Should Britain remain a monarchy?

It seems unlikely that Britain will become a republic any time soon; in fact, the popularity of the royal family has increased in recent years. This is partly due to the younger generation of royals led by Prince William and Prince Harry, who work hard to engage with people on a personal level. However, there are still plenty of people who believe the monarchy should be abolished:

Arguments for keeping the monarchy

- The Queen is a neutral head of state → not involved in politics or chosen by one particular political party.
- She stands for British values and national unity.
- She is an integral part of the nation's culture and heritage.
- She represents British interests abroad and improves international relations, both by travelling to other countries and by receiving visiting heads of state in Britain.
- It is better to have an unelected head of state who does not need the support of particular interest groups.
- A monarch brings stability, unlike a president who changes every few years
- The royal family does a lot of good through charity work.
- The Queen and the rest of the royal family attract tourists, who contribute a lot of money to the British economy.

Arguments for abolishing the monarchy

- The monarchy is an old-fashioned institution that is no longer needed in the 21st century.
- A monarch is undemocratic: the people should be able to elect their head of state.
- An elected head of state can be held accountable for their actions; a monarch could misuse their status if they wanted to.
- A royal family reinforces the idea that some people are born better than others and that the citizens of the country need to be ruled.
- The royal family is very expensive, e.g. in terms of providing security for them → taxes could be better spent on other things.
- Tourists would come to Britain anyway: they do not only come because of the royal family.

Republicans in Britain

"Republic", an organisation that campaigns to abolish the monarchy, would like to hold a referendum on the monarchy after Queen Elizabeth II dies. They believe this would be a good time because:

- A lot of support for the royal family is actually loyalty to the Queen.
- Since she has been on the throne for so long (67 years), a large number of British people have never known another head of state, and have therefore never really thought about making a change.
- It will open up public debate on whether a hereditary head of state makes sense in today's society.

Abi Tipp

DON'T MIX THEM UP!

"Britain" is not the same as "England"!

- Great Britain: the main island, consisting of England, Scotland and Wales
- The United Kingdom of Great Britain and Northern Ireland: the official political name
- The British Isles: the main island, along with Ireland and several smaller islands such as the Shetlands

Citizens are "British", but many also identify themselves by the country of their birth, i.e. English, Irish, Scottish or Welsh.

British society

Social institutions and services

Before the welfare state

- Until the early 20th century, poor people had to rely on their families, churches and other charities for help.
- Those in desperate need were sent to a workhouse → provided very basic food and shelter in return for manual labour.
- The conditions there were so terrible that needy people did whatever they could to avoid being sent there.

1905–1911

- The Liberal government introduced public services to take away the shame of poverty.
- These included old age pensions, free school meals, labour exchanges (where the unemployed could find available jobs).

The Beveridge Report (1942)

- The report recommended the introduction of a national insurance scheme to fund healthcare, education and financial benefits for families.
- All workers were to contribute to this insurance.
- In 1948 the National Health Service (NHS) was founded, the first scheme of its kind in the world. It gave every citizen access to free healthcare.

The NHS today

- Every British citizen has the right to free treatment by a local doctor.
- The system is very expensive: patients now have to pay for some services, e.g. dental or eye care.
- Treatment remains free for certain groups, e.g. children under 16 and people on low incomes.
- NHS hospitals vary greatly in terms of conditions for the patients and services available.
- There can be long waiting lists for routine, non-urgent operations.

- Many people now have private health insurance; however, even people with private insurance must continue to pay national insurance contributions.

Other features of the welfare state

Social security

- Also known as "benefits", social security is financial aid for needy people.
- It includes unemployment benefit, housing benefit and state pensions (for retired people).

Social services

- Care of elderly and disabled people, in their own home or in a nursing home
- Care for children and young people whose own families cannot care for them
- Child protection services
- Care for the mentally ill

Pros and cons of a welfare state

British citizens are lucky to live in a country that provides help for them if they are in need. However, opinion is divided on how much help the state should provide:

Arguments for the welfare state	Arguments against the welfare state
Many people are needy for reasons beyond their control → they may have lost their job or are disabled and cannot work → it is the duty of the state to support them.	Individuals should be responsible for their own lives → should not rely on handouts from the state.
It is fair to redistribute a society's wealth → even people who cannot pay into the system have the right to financial help.	If help is easily available, people become lazy and do not try to look for work.
Social problems would increase without the welfare state → people might turn to crime to feed their families or become homeless.	The system is too expensive → the state cannot afford to support large numbers of people.

Arguments for the welfare state	Arguments against the welfare state
Humanitarianism: it is our moral duty as a society to take care of people who cannot help themselves.	Charities are there to help the needy → support does not have to come from the state.

Britain as a class society

The British are very class-conscious. Although today the different social classes are more flexible, the differences are still noticeable.

Abi Tipp

WATCH OUT FOR STEREOTYPES!

→ Note that some ways used to identify a person's social class are generalisations and/or stereotypes – do not take them too literally!

→ They serve more as a general guideline to class differences

Ways of identifying a person's social class:

Upper classes

- "posh" accent; "Oxford English"; received pronunciation
- attended a public school, e.g. Eton; Oxford or Cambridge University
- home: large, detached house, possibly in the countryside
- many upper-class, Oxbridge graduates have high-level jobs in the government and industry
- expensive holidays abroad
- read the "quality" newspapers, e.g. the Times

Middle classes

- fairly neutral accent, possibly with a regional touch
- attended grammar school or an independent school; redbrick universities
- home: often in green, suburban areas
- jobs: higher management; professionals such as doctors or teachers
- foreign holidays
- read papers like the *Guardian* or the *Independent*

Lower classes

- often have a strong regional accent
- attended their local comprehensive school; often do not go to university
- home: housing estates; block of flats; small terraced house
- jobs: public services; retail; semi-skilled workers, unskilled workers
- cheap package holidays
- read tabloids such as the *Sun* or the *Daily Mail*

Class and wealth

- In the past, wealth was a good indication of a person's class.
- The upper classes were rich due to inherited money.
- The middle classes were e.g. factory owners who also had plenty of money.
- Nowadays, money is no longer such an accurate indication of class:

→ People from lower/working class backgrounds can get a well-paying job, or even win a large amount of money.

→ However, how a person chooses to spend their money can still be an indication of their social class.

Immigration and ethnic minorities in Britain

IMMIGRATION TO BRITAIN

→ Around 1in 8 people living in Britain were born in another country

→ Largest immigrant groups: from Asia, especially the Indian sub-continent, the Caribbean, and Europe

→ Main reasons for immigration: work, study, to seek asylum, to join family members

Immigrants from former colonies

- 1950s and 1960s: urgent need for workers in the UK = invited people from former colonies (Caribbean, India, Pakistan) to come
- As citizens of Commonwealth countries, they were given a residence permit for the UK.
- high unemployment among this group during the economic downturn in the 1970s

Immigrants from former colonies

Immigrants from the European Union

- EU citizens have the right to live and work in any other member country as long as they have a job or enough money to live off.
- large fall in number of EU citizens moving to Britain since the Brexit vote
- many have also left the UK due to uncertainty about their future status after Brexit → many now feel unwelcome
- fears of a "brain drain" of specialists from EU countries = would cause problems for British industry in the future

Refugees and asylum seekers

- number of asylum seekers increased sharply at the end of the 1980s = people from Somalia and former Yugoslavia
- Fewer people seek asylum in Britain today = the number of people allowed to do so is limited to around 25,000 per year.
- Civil war in Syria since 2011: refugee crisis in Europe → many migrants reached France and tried to cross to Britain through the Channel Tunnel.
- Anti-refugee propaganda is widespread: tabloid newspapers and parties such as UKIP stir up public opinion against refugees.

Britain as a multicultural society

ETHNIC BACKGROUND OF THE UK POPULATION:

The main ethnic groups in Britain today:

→ White
→ Indian
→ Black African
→ Black Caribbean
→ Pakistani
→ Bangladeshi
→ Chinese
→ Mixed race

Is a multicultural society good or bad?

Arguments for a multicultural society

- Ethnic diversity enriches a society.
- Ethnic food becomes part of the culture, e.g. British love of curry.
- More tolerance due to interaction with different kinds of people
- More people are in relationships with someone from another culture → promotes understanding on a personal level.
- Multiculturalism can lead to a more peaceful society = people are more accepting of differences, unlike isolationist countries that are not used to foreigners and therefore more suspicious and intolerant.

Arguments against a multicultural society

- A country's national identity and traditions will be lost if they become too diluted with those of other cultures.
- When cultures are very different, they cannot integrate → only exist side by side.
- Many immigrants do not want to integrate into British society → they create division.
- People from different cultures do not always share the same values as the rest of society → can lead to racial tension.
- People who do not identify with their host country can become isolated → they only live within their own communities.

Problems facing migrants in Britain

- Integration can be difficult, especially if they do not speak English.
- Many have low-paid, unskilled jobs.
- Many live in inner city areas with poor housing.
- They are faced with discrimination → some people believe they have only come to Britain to get social security payments and free healthcare.
- There are not many members of ethnic minorities in politics, the police force, the army and similar fields → hard to identify with authority figures.
- Increase in anti-Islam sentiment in recent years = due to increase in terrorist attacks by Islamic extremists.
- Muslims or "Muslim-looking" people face additional discrimination.

Second-generation migrants

Children born in Britain to migrant parents often find themselves in a difficult position:

- They live with **two cultures**: their family's culture in the home with its traditions and beliefs, and, outside the home, the same Western culture that their classmates and friends share.
- This can lead to a **culture clash**.
- They can feel **distanced** from their parents' and grandparents' culture → they may not speak their language and may never have visited their parents' home country.
- They feel they have to **live up to their parents' expectations** → some feel guilty about trying to lead their own life.
- They might face **discrimination** → they are seen as foreign, when in fact they feel British.
- They experience a **crisis of identity** → they do not completely belong to either culture.

Some migrant parents also find it difficult to identify with their children, and might be disappointed if those children do not embrace their culture. They have emigrated to provide a better life for their family but their children might not understand or appreciate their sacrifice.

Britain and the world

THE BRITISH EMPIRE

- → Lasted from the late 16th – mid-20th century
- → Largest empire that has ever existed
- → Comprised over 20 % of the world's land area and about 458 million people at its height (early 1900s)
- → "The sun never sets on the British Empire" = the empire was so extensive that there would always be daylight in at least one of the colonies.

The beginnings of the Empire

- Britain is an island → explored the world **by sea.**
- First main explorations:
  1588: Francis Drake sailed around the world.
  1578–1595: Walter Raleigh explored the Americas.
- **First long-term colonies** founded at beginning of **17th century**
- From the start, **economic factors** played an important role.
- Britain wanted to **increase its wealth** through foreign trade.
- The colonies were a source of **cheap raw materials** and a market for exports.
- Large trading companies were established, e.g.:
  the East India Company (1600),
  the London (Virginia) Company (1606).

The first empire

The first British colonies were in:

- the West Indies (Jamaica, the Bahamas, Bermuda)
- India (was not directly ruled by Britain until 1858)
- North America
- Canada (Newfoundland, Hudson Bay)
- Gibraltar

Britain acquired some of this land during wars with France (Canada, India) and Spain (West Indies, Gibraltar). After gaining control of Gibraltar, Britain was allowed to supply slaves and trade goods in the Spanish Americas, establishing itself as a major overseas power.

The North American colonies

These consisted of three main groups:

- The **New England Colonies** = the area around Boston settled by the Puritans
- The **Middle Colonies** = the area around New York settled by various European immigrants looking for religious and political freedom
- The **Southern Colonies** = Maryland, Virginia, North and South Carolina and Georgia. **Tobacco** and **cotton** were grown here; **slavery** was introduced

Loss of the North American colonies:

- 18th century: the British empire was growing = becoming more expensive to run.
- Britain decided to impose **taxes** on the North American colonies = the **Stamp Act** (1765)
- The colonists resisted = they did not want to pay tax because they were not represented in the British Parliament
- 1773: the **Boston Tea Party** was a protest against tea taxes.
- led to the **War of Independence** and the foundation of the **United States of America** as a nation in its own right.

The second empire

After America became independent, Britain concentrated on expanding its empire towards the east.

- **Trade** still played the most important role in this expansion.
- During the **Industrial Revolution**, there was a huge increase in goods available for export and in the need for raw materials.
- The new colonies contributed significantly to Britain's **wealth.**
- These colonies made Britain a **world power.**

THE RISE OF IMPERALISM

- → As the empire expanded, the colonists saw it as their mission to "civilise" the native populations.
- → Western values, beliefs and many aspects of white society were considered best for the local people.
- → This was often done with a lack of sensitivity, leading to resentment and resistance.
- → The colonised countries ultimately fought for independence.

Overview of some important British colonies

Australia
• Explored by Captain Cook in the 1770s → he brought home reports of a large, fertile land that could form a valuable part of the empire. • At first it was used as a penal colony to ease some of the pressure on Britain's overcrowded prisons. • When gold was discovered there, it became a source of wealth for Britain and a destination for people wanting to make their fortune. • After this, it no longer made sense to send people there as a punishment. • Australia became one of the main British colonies for European settlers, along with New Zealand and Canada.
Africa
• The British gained a stronghold in South Africa in the early 19th century when they conquered Cape Colony from the Dutch. • By the start of the 20th century, Britain controlled one third of the African continent. • A "Cape to Cairo" railway was suggested to link the mineral-rich colonies in the south (gold, diamonds) with the north → the British controlled part of the Suez Canal there. • The Canal was strategically important to the British Empire = fast link to the east and better trade routes.

The break-up of the Empire

Reasons for the end of colonisation

- Australia, New Zealand and Canada: demanded the right to govern themselves
- Rebellions in India against the colonial rulers (Great Sepoy Mutiny in 1857, passive resistance led by Mahatma Gandhi from 1920)
- Growing nationalism and demands for independence, e.g. in Ireland from 1916, Kenya in 1952)
- Citizens of British colonies were conscripted to fight for Britain during the two World Wars – the colonies did not agree to this.
- Running colonies was expensive – some were given independence (e.g. Egypt) to ease the financial strain on Britain.

British Overseas Territories today

Fourteen territories around the world remain part of Britain today. They include:

- Bermuda
- the Cayman Islands
- the Falkland Islands
- Gibraltar
- some Caribbean islands, e.g. Monserrat

They are self-governing but depend on Britain for defence and foreign affairs

Unexpected problems:

- In 1982, the **Falkland Islands** were seized by Argentina (which claims the islands are Argentinian). Britain regained control of the Falklands after two months of costly war.
- The future of **Gibraltar** after Brexit remains unclear. It will have to leave the EU when Britain does, although most of its citizens voted to remain.
- In addition to this, Spain claims that Gibraltar is Spanish and wants to govern the state jointly with Britain.

POST-COLONIAL SOCIETIES

- → not easy for former colonies to adapt after gaining independence
- → They had been forced to adopt British values → very different from their own.
- → Newly independent states now had to search for their identity and recreate forgotten traditions.
- → Identity crisis: people who had grown up under British rule did not really feel part of their own culture, but not really British, either.
- → Political instability: citizens had to get used to voting for and being governed by their own people.
- → Some former colonies were left economically weaker.

Focus on India: during and after British rule

Timeline of British rule:

- 16th century: the British **East India Tea Company** was founded → trade in tea, spices and cotton.
- The British started to play an **active role in Indian politics** in order to consolidate their position there.
- The East India Company had its own army, which **conquered large parts of India** and acted as an administrator for the Indian subcontinent.
- 1857–1858: the **Indian Rebellion** (also known as the **Sepoy Mutiny**, or **Indian Mutiny**) → an unsuccessful attempt to regain control of the territories governed by the East India Company.
- 1858: after **suppressing the rebellion**, the British Crown took control of the Indian subcontinent → beginning of the **Raj.**
- English became the **official language** of India.
- 1876: Queen Victoria was pronounced **Empress of India.**
- 1937: **Burma** became a separate colony within the Indian Empire → gained independence in 1948.
- 1947: India became an **independent country** → it was divided into the **Union of India** and the **Dominion of Pakistan.**

Problems following independence:

- Many people disagreed with the **partition** of the Indian Empire → led to riots.
- The Union of India was mainly **Hindu** and the Dominion of Pakistan mainly **Muslim** → fear of religious persecution led to mass migration as people tried to move from one state to the other.

- Result: millions of **homeless** people and at least half a million **killed**
- Two regions in the north-west, **Jammu** (mostly Hindu) and **Kashmir** (mostly Muslim), were claimed by both India and Pakistan.
- At the time of independence, these regions were **ruled by a Maharajah** → these local rulers were allowed to choose which country to join.
- The Maharajah of Jammu and Kashmir chose to **join India.**
- This is still a **matter of dispute** between India and Pakistan today.
- Pakistan believes the two regions should join their nation as most citizens are Muslim.
- India believes the Maharajah's decision should be final and the regions should remain part of India.

India today

What is modern-day India like, 70 years after gaining independence?

Positive aspects

- India has the 7th largest economy in the world, which is expected to grow even faster in the next 30 years.
- huge growth in the fields of information technology, financial services and telecommunications
- increase in the number of children attending primary school → three-quarters of the population are now literate
- The caste system (= strict separation of people into social classes), which played a huge role in Indian society, has become more flexible → positive discrimination allows people from lower castes to get a better education and have jobs that were forbidden to them in the past.
- Well-educated women can achieve equal status to men → India has one of the highest number of female politicians in the world, and has had a female president (Pratibha Patil) and female prime minister (Indira Gandhi).
- The film industry has grown significantly and "Bollywood" films have become popular around the world, raising India's international profile.

Negative aspects

- There is a very wide gap between rich and poor → nearly 30 % of people live below the poverty line.
- Not all children in rural areas go to school.
- Girls are more likely than boys to be illiterate.
- Women are often still treated as second-class citizens, particularly in rural areas → girls can be forced to marry at a young age; rape often goes unpunished; women are victims of acid attacks, where acid is thrown at them as a punishment for disobeying their husband in some way, or for disrespecting their family.
- Problems with overpopulation and the negative effect this has on the environment.
- The rapid economic growth also has a negative effect on the environment → increase in air and water pollution.

Clearly, India has made a great deal of progress since gaining independence from Britain, and has become one of the world's strongest economic forces. However, poverty and inequality are still widespread, problems that are not easy to solve in a country with such a large population.

The British Commonwealth

Many of Britain's former colonies remain part of an organisation called the **Commonwealth of Nations**.

- At first, it was a way of maintaining economic ties with former colonies
- Today: the member states can interact on a more informal level.
- The states initially had a lot in common, e.g. language and culture, due to their former ties to Britain.

Foundation of the Commonwealth

- 1931: The Commonwealth of Nations was established as an association of all British dominions.
- These states now had the right to reject any laws passed by the British government and to pass their own laws on domestic affairs.
- Former colonies that had become republics (e.g. India) and therefore did not recognise the Queen as head of state, joined the Commonwealth at a later stage.
- For them, the British monarch was the symbolic head of the Commonwealth but not of their own country.
- Economic ties and trade between Commonwealth countries remained important.

The Commonwealth today

- There are 52 members states including Britain.
- The heads of government or state meet at regular intervals to discuss international issues.
- There are many Commonwealth institutes, societies, professional associations and university exchange programmes.
- The Commonwealth Games, a large sporting event, are held every four years. The athletes compete in a wide variety of sports, including some that are only really played in Commonwealth countries, such as netball and lawn bowls.
- There are joint British/Commonwealth programmes in agriculture, engineering, health and education.
- Commonwealth citizens get privileges that are not available to all foreigners. These include the right to vote or to participate in certain immigration programmes.

Principles of the Commonwealth

- 1971 Singapore Declaration: commitment to peace, equality and fighting racism, as well as economic and social development
- 1991 Harare Declaration: focus on democracy, human rights and social justice
- Commonwealth mission statement: emphasizes the importance of mutual respect, peace and prosperity for member states; promotes equality, diversity and shared values

- Member states that violate these principles can be punished with economic sanctions or even suspension from the Commonwealth.
- For example, Zimbabwe was suspended in 2002 due to land reform policies and human rights violations under the leadership of President Mugabe.
- Membership is voluntary, and member states are free to leave if they wish to.

The future of the Commonwealth

- It is difficult to say whether the Commonwealth has a future in the long term.
- Economic ties with Britain weakened over time as the importance of the European Union grew.
- However, following Brexit, the British government has said it wants to increase trade again within the Commonwealth.
- In 2011, the Commonwealth was accused of not taking enough action against human rights violations committed by its members → the lack of interest among the member states was seen as a sign that the Commonwealth may be coming to the end of its natural life.
- The traditional sense of solidarity among Commonwealth countries has been lost: many of them no longer have much in common with each other.

Britain and Europe

RELATIONSHIP WITH EUROPE

- → often an uneasy relationship
- → Britain as an island is physically separate from mainland Europe.
- → Britain developed close ties with more distant countries due to the Empire.
- → special relationship with the USA: common language and culture

Post-war Britain

The Second World War change the balance of world power → in many ways, Britain could no longer keep up:

- It needed financial help from the USA and Canada because it was so badly in debt.
- There were shortages and rationing of food and everyday goods → food rationing did not end until 1954.
- There was a lack of housing.
- Many of its colonies wanted independence = the end of the Empire
- The new world powers were the USA and the USSR.

European division and unity

- Europe was **rebuilt from two sides** and in two very different ways following World War II.
- The Western countries followed a **capitalist, democratic** ideology
- The Eastern bloc took on the **Communism** of the USSR

Some Western countries felt they could become strong again, both **economically** and **politically**, if they formed some kind of union.

- They wanted to **prevent another war.**
- It was a way of **boosting the economies** of European countries.

However, Britain felt that its political ties were **closer to the USA**.

- Britain joined **NATO** in 1949.
- Did not become a member of the **European Community** (EC) until 1973.

Key dates

- 1975: in a referendum, two-thirds of Britons voted to remain in the EC, despite huge opposition when the country first joined.
- 1991: although Britain signed the Maastricht Treaty that enabled the start of the single European market, Prime Minister John Major made sure Britain had the option of remaining outside the single currency.
- Major did not sign the Social Charter that guaranteed certain minimum conditions of employment through the EC.
- 2002: Britain, along with Denmark and Sweden, did not change its currency to the euro when the other 12 member states at the time did so.

Abi Tipp

KEEP UP-TO-DATE!

In politics, things can change quickly. To make sure you are up-to-date on developing issues such as Brexit, scroll through online resources such as bbc.co.uk once or twice a week.

BREXIT – SHOULD BRITAIN LEAVE THE EU?

→ Controversial issue that has divided the country deeply
→ In a referendum held on 23 June 2016, Britain voted to leave the EU by a margin of just 52 %.
→ The official process to leave was started in March 2017, initially giving Britain 2 years to work out the logistics of leaving.

Arguments for Brexit	Arguments against Brexit
Leaving the EU will allow Britain to control immigration and reduce the number of immigrants entering the country → EU citizens will no longer have an automatic right to live there.	Leaving the EU will not solve immigration problems. Instead, it will bring them closer, because border controls with Europe that are now in Calais, France, will be moved to Dover, England.
Britain would have more freedom to make important trade deals with countries such as India or China → doing most of its trade within Europe is too limiting.	Nearly half of Britain's exports go to the EU, so leaving the free trade zone would have a negative effect.

Arguments for Brexit	Arguments against Brexit
Britain is forced to pass a lot of laws that have been made in Europe → British courts should get their sovereignty back and only deal with laws concerning British interests.	There are not many laws that are determined by the European Commission. In addition to this, British citizens will suffer if Britain no longer has to comply with certain laws, such as those on human rights.
Jobs will not really be affected → Britain can easily develop a strong market after Brexit.	Around 3 million jobs are linked to the EU → these jobs will have an uncertain future, because businesses will be less likely to invest in a country outside Europe.
Britain does not need the EU to be influential on the world stage.	British interests are best protected as part of the EU bloc.
International banks will not leave London and take their headquarters elsewhere. They will stay and take advantage of low tax rates.	Banks will leave the UK because there are greater advantages of trading within the EU.
The British Parliament must become sovereign again → this can only happen without being tied closely to Europe.	It is important that countries work closely together in today's globalised world.

TALKING POINTS: BRITAIN

Checkliste

Make sure you can answer the following questions on Britain!

→ What are the two chambers of the British parliament called?
→ Which countries have their own parliaments?
→ What are the arguments for and against Scottish independence?
→ What role does the monarch play in Britain today?
→ What are the arguments for and against the monarchy?
→ What are the reasons for and against having a welfare state?
→ What differences can be seen between the classes in Britain?
→ Why do people emigrate to Britain?
→ Is a multicultural society a good or bad thing?
→ Outline the rise and fall of the British Empire.
→ What challenges are faced by a post-colonial society?
→ What are the arguments for and against Brexit?

5 TALKING POINTS: USA

Politics in the USA

Political system

The political system in the United States is made up of three parts:

- the Legislative Branch,
- the Executive Branch,
- the Judicial Branch.

Legislative Branch

- Consists of **Congress**, which is divided into two chambers: the **House of Representatives** and the **Senate**
- Both chambers have equal power.
- Both are elected directly by the citizens of the USA.
- Both must agree before a bill can become law.

The powers of Congress include:

- making laws,
- imposing and collecting taxes, and controlling federal spending,
- printing money and regulating its value,
- overseeing and checking the activities of the Executive Branch.

Executive Branch

The Executive Branch consists of the President and Vice President of the United States and an organisation of around four million people, including one million military staff.

- In order to be elected president, candidates must have been born in the USA, be at least 35 years of age and have lived in the US for at least 14 years.
- Until the election of Barack Obama in 2008, all US presidents were white males.
- A president serves a four-year term of office and cannot serve more than two terms overall.
- He and the Vice President are elected by the Electoral College (see below), and are the only political figures to be elected nationally, all other elections taking place at state or district level.

THE ROLE OF THE PRESIDENT

- → Head of State, Head of Government, military Commander-in-Chief and Chief Diplomat
- → suggests new laws to Congress
- → signs or vetoes laws passed by Congress
- → appoints federal judges (including Supreme Court judges) → these must be approved by the Senate
- → appoints members of the Cabinet, federal agencies (e.g. the CIA) and other federal employees → also need Senate approval
- → manages national affairs and the federal government
- → influences foreign policy
- → controls military strategy and matters of national security

Judicial Branch

The USA has two types of courts: the **federal** courts and the courts of each individual **state**. The final court of appeal is the **Supreme Court**.

State courts

- Each state in America has its own laws and legal procedures.
- They deal with civil cases involving private individuals, or cases between citizens and local or state governments.
- Each state has its own supreme court, which has the final say in matters concerning that particular state's laws and constitution, and is the final court of appeal in such matters.
- However, if the case involves national rather than state issues, it may be taken to a federal court on appeal.

Federal system: the Supreme Court

- This is the highest court in the land, where the final judgements are given.
- The court has nine judges who are nominated by the President, subject to approval by the Senate.
- The appointment of judges can be controversial, as the President is likely to choose people who are sympathetic to his views. This can then have an effect on the judgements that are passed, although the judges should, theoretically, be neutral.

- The most important job for the Supreme Court is to rule on whether certain laws or government policies are unconstitutional or not. In so doing, it can overrule decisions made by the government.
- All federal courts must follow the rulings made by the Supreme Court in matters concerning the Constitution and federal laws.

Abi Tipp

GOOD TO KNOW:

Why is the US political system made up of three parts?

- When working out the terms of government following independence, the authors of the Constitution were afraid of corruption.
- They therefore introduced this "system of checks and balances" = each branch of government has some control over the other 2.
- Prevents one branch from becoming too strong.

THE AMERICAN CONSTITUTION

→ Considered one of the great political documents of the Western world.
→ It was formulated in 1787 and ratified in 1788 following the War of Independence from Britain.
→ The Constitution forms the basis of government in the US.

The US Constitution – the most important aspects

- The citizens have the power to elect the people who govern them.
- Politicians answer to the people who elected them, and are responsible for their needs.
- the separation of powers
- the system of checks and balances
- Federalism: both the national government and the individual states share authority to govern = neither one can become more powerful than the other.
- Flexibility = amendments can be made to the Constitution if and when they become necessary.

The Bill of Rights

The first ten amendments to the Constitution were added in **1791** and are known collectively as the **Bill of Rights**. They set down certain civil rights that every citizen should have, including:

- freedom of speech, the press and religion,
- the right to hold meetings as long as they are peaceful,
- the right to own and use weapons for protection,
- the right to a fair trial, and freedom from cruel and unusual punishment.

The political parties in the US

The USA is basically a two-party state, with:

- the **Democratic Party** and
- the **Republican Party**.

There are some smaller parties, such as the **Green Party**, but they tend to have more success at **local or state level**.

- **All seats in Congress except two** are currently held by either Republicans or Democrats.
- The remaining two seats are held by independent candidates.

Overview of the two main parties

The Democratic Party

generally in favour of	generally against
a higher minimum wage	the free availability of guns
more government money for health-care; possibly a national health system	the use of torture against prisoners
more investment in alternative and renewable energy sources	climate change denial
a reasonable minimum wage	violations of the right to privacy
affordable higher education for everyone	the death penalty
equal opportunities and affirmative action = more diversity e.g. in the workplace	lower taxes for rich people
same-sex marriage and rights for LGBTQ people	discrimination against people with physical or mental disabilities
the right of access to birth control and abortion	withdrawal of American troops from e.g. Iraq

The Republican Party

generally in favour of	generally against
free-market policies = companies should be able to run their own business without government interference	easy access to welfare benefits = people should not be encouraged to accept hand-outs from the state
tax cuts, especially for people who create jobs	an increase in the minimum wage
capital punishment	a national health insurance scheme
the right to own guns	forming trade unions so that workers have some protection from unfair practices
stricter anti-terrorism laws	drugs, including "recreational drugs" such as marijuana
stricter immigration laws	affirmative action for minorities and women
traditional family values	LGBTQ rights

ELECTION CAMPAIGNS

- Elections are a big part of American politics.
- new president every 4 years; Congressional elections every 2 years
- A lot of money is spent on election campaigns → personal appearances by celebrities and extensive use of the media.
- The idea of television debates between presidential candidates originated in America.

How presidential candidates are chosen

- Some states hold primary elections → the candidates are chosen by the voters.
- Or the candidate is chosen at a party convention, where party members choose delegates for selection as presidential candidate.

The Electoral College

What is the Electoral College?

- The President and Vice President are elected indirectly through this system.
- In the early years of the USA, many people lived in rural areas and didn't know much about the candidates.
- Communications were poor and it was difficult for candidates to travel and meet the people.
- It was also thought that ordinary, often uneducated people, were not capable of choosing a good president.
- Local people were nominated as "electors" to represent the candidates.
- The other local citizens voted for one of these electors → they then gave their votes to the candidate of their own choice.

Religion in the USA

RELIGIOUS BEGINNINGS

- Many early European settlers had left their home country for religious reasons.
- They were being persecuted for their beliefs.
- They were looking for a place to practice their religion freely.
- Many of their beliefs and principles formed the foundation of the present-day USA.

The Puritans

- 1620: A group that came to be known as the Pilgrim Fathers were Protestant dissenters who had broken with the Church of England.
- They decided to start a new colony in North America where they could worship in their own way and maintain their cultural identity.
- Their ship was called the Mayflower, and their settlement was the Plymouth Colony.

The Puritans

- The original colonists survived in this new, unfamiliar territory with help from local Native Americans, who showed them how to grow and gather food.
- From 1630: The Puritans were Protestants who aimed to "purify" the Church of England of practices left over from the days before the spilt with the Roman Catholic Church → they wanted their church to be simple and "pure", without hierarchies.
- The Puritans first settled in Massachusetts, and then spread throughout the new colonies → they were intolerant of anyone who did not share their religious beliefs.
- 1636: Roger Williams, a Puritan leader, was forced to leave Massachusetts because of his disagreements with the colonial government there.
- He founded a colony of his own in Rhode Island, based on principles of religious freedom rather than forced worship.
- Some of these principles, such as the separation of church and state, religious tolerance and freedom of religion, were written into the American Constitution.

Abi Tipp

GOOD TO KNOW: SEPARATION OF CHURCH AND STATE

In the USA, there is no official state religion. It is also illegal to prevent people from practising a particular religion. However, religion often has a strong influence on e.g. politics and education, although, officially, it should not.

The Puritan legacy

The American mentality today owes a lot to the nation's Puritan beginnings:

- The concept of the **"Protestant work ethic"**, i.e. that hard work and self-discipline lead to success, plays an important role in the American business world.
- The Puritans believed that they were very special in God's eyes, and that **God had blessed their new country**. They therefore felt they had a **moral right to defend their beliefs** and way of life.

- In addition to this, they believed strongly in a **fair and equal society**, and refused to tolerate anyone who did not share their views on what that society should be like.
- Some people see this way of thinking reflected in America's perspective today: Americans believe their society is the **best in the world**, and it is difficult for them to imagine why anyone would think otherwise.
- It was thought that **personal wealth** was a sign of God's blessing, which is one reason why making a lot of money is seen as a virtue.
- However, the Puritans also believed that it was their **duty to help the needy**; Americans today are very generous when it comes to works of charity.

Religion in the USA today

Different religions

- The majority of Americans identify as **Christian**.
- These include **Protestants** (the largest group) and **Catholics**, but also **Mormons** or **Jehovah's Witnesses**.
- There are also several **black churches** (e.g. African Methodist Episcopal Church).
- The **Bible Belt** = southern states such as Arkansas, Mississippi, Alabama, Tennessee, North and South Carolina, Kentucky → home to large number of evangelical Protestants who live in close accordance to the teachings of the Bible.
- The term is associated with very conservative attitudes.
- Other faiths in the USA include **Judaism, Islam, Buddhism** and **Hinduism**.

Muslims in the USA

- There are an estimated six to seven million Muslims in the USA, most of whom are well-integrated into American life.
- However, there has been a sharp increase in anti-Islam feeling in recent years.
- American Muslims often have to face greater discrimination and stereotyping.
- Most Muslim organisations in the States emphasize their moderate standpoint, and strongly condemn any form of terrorism.

Religion and politics

Although state and religion are separate according to the Constitution, the influence of certain religious groups on political issues is very strong:

- Except for John F. Kennedy, who was a Catholic, and Barack Obama, who is African American, all American presidents have been **WASPs (White Anglo-Saxon Protestants)**.
- Nearly three-quarters of Republicans today belong to a **white Christian religious group** → around 35 % say belong to an **evangelical church.**
- The more fundamentalist of these believe strongly in **traditional family values**, no sex outside of marriage, and the traditional role of the woman in the home → they want their elected politicians to reflect these values.
- These groups **oppose**, among other things, **homosexuality, abortion, euthanasia** and certain kinds of biotechnology, such as **human cloning** and **stem cell research**.
- All of these are political issues in the US.
- Many would like to **ban contraceptives**.
- Since the 1970s, groups belonging to the **Christian Right** have influenced voters = they want to hit back against liberal government policies.

Religion and education

The question of evolution

- Controversial issue: should evolution be taught in schools as scientific fact or as just one possible explanation of how our planet came to exist?
- In some states, particularly in the Bible Belt, fundamentalist and family values pressure groups do not want pupils to be taught about evolution as fact. Instead, they favour one of two alternative explanations about the origins of the world:

→ **Creationism** = a literal interpretation of the Bible, which states that God created the world in seven days no more than 10,000 years ago. Not all Creationists believe in this timeframe, but all think that evolution cannot adequately explain how the Earth came to exist.

The question of evolution

→ **Intelligent design** = the idea that all biological developments happened for a reason, and that the natural world was "designed" by an external being, i.e. God, in order to arrive at our current point of development.

- As a result of such pressure groups, some states, such as Georgia, had a sticker placed in the front of school science textbooks which stated:

→ "This textbook contains material on evolution. Evolution is a theory, not a fact, regarding the origin of living things. This material should be approached with an open mind, studied carefully, and critically considered."

- In 2006, a group of parents in Georgia won a court case in which they sued their local school district to have the sticker removed.

SCHOOL CURRICULA: THE STATE DECIDES

→ Because each state is free to develop its own education system and curriculum, there are no national guidelines on what should or should not be taught.

→ This makes it easier for pressure groups to have an effect at a local level.

Sex education in schools

- Many parents from conservative religious backgrounds support "abstinence-only" sex education → children are taught that they should not have sex unless they are married.
- These parents feel that teaching young people about issues such as contraception encourages them to become sexually active at a younger age.
- Others worry that their children will be taught things that do not match their family's views on the subject.
- However, studies have shown that abstinence-only teaching does not reduce the number of sexually active teenagers or unplanned pregnancies.
- At the same time, young people are missing out on vital information on sexual health → they do not know about birth control, safe sex or sexually transmitted diseases.

America: the land of opportunity

THE AMERICAN DREAM

- From the outset, America was seen as the land of opportunity = a place of freedom where a person could become anything they wanted to be.
- Originally the focus was on social improvement rather than becoming rich.
- There was to be a fair society in which everyone was equal and could fulfil their potential.
- From the mid-19th century the focus was more on material gain → the California Gold Rush showed that the dream of becoming extremely rich could come true.
- The social aspects of equality gradually lost their importance.

The dream of "rags to riches"

- The idea that anyone prepared to work hard enough can go **"from rags to riches"** is still part of the American mindset.
- The concept was fuelled by the huge **increase in American's economic power** from the mid-19th century onwards:
- **Manufacturing** greatly increased due to the discovery of the country's natural resources (e.g. **coal and iron**), in combination with plentiful **cheap labour** in the form of immigrants → Manufacturers became extremely wealthy.
- The **age of invention**: many new products, such as telephones, elevators and fridges, were either invented or developed in the US.
- Manufacturing processes were made easier and more efficient through **electricity** and **mass production**, made possible by the invention of the **assembly line** → goods could be produced faster and more cheaply.
- The development of the **railways** meant that goods could be distributed around the country quickly and easily.
- This meant it really was possible to start with a small idea, work hard, and become extremely wealthy.

Today, most people have little chance of fulfilling the American Dream:

- In theory, it is still possible to work your way up from nothing.
- However, the gap between rich and poor is wider than ever.

- It is difficult to break away from poverty.
- For example: it is very expensive to go to university in the US, making it difficult for people from deprived backgrounds to get the kind of education which would help them advance in the world.

MANIFEST DESTINY

- → The term was coined in 1839.
- → Few people lived in the central and western parts of the US.
- → The government wanted to secure the USA's status as a nation by settling the whole country.
- → They believed God was calling them to establish a great nation = it was their "manifest", or clear, destiny to push back the frontier until it reached the Pacific Ocean.

The frontier

- Many families, known as pioneers, were encouraged to head west to make a new life for themselves.
- They established American settlements, with American values, across the expanse of North America.
- Later, America continued to look for new frontiers to conquer → e.g. space exploration.

Manifest Destiny and patriotism

- American patriotism is closely linked to the concept of Manifest Destiny and the frontier.
- Expanding its territory to the west helped to fulfil America's destiny of becoming the world's greatest nation.
- Americans believe their values are the best and should be spread around the world.
- Americans have to be the best at all their undertakings. This was a driving force behind the race to be the first to land on the moon: it was vital for American pride that they should beat the Russians at this landmark achievement.
- American pride took a knock during the Vietnam War, in which they were defeated by a Communist country → many people, especially young people, questioned whether the war was just and demonstrated against the government.

- The terrorist attacks of 9 September 2001 reunited Americans in support of their country and against anyone who dared to attack it.
- Donald Trump exploited patriotic feelings during his 2016 presidential campaign by pledging to "make America great again".

Immigration in the USA

Seen as the land of opportunity, America has always been a **popular destination for immigrants from all over the world**. Immigrants come from all over the world. The ethnic mix also includes Native Americans and descendants of African slaves. There have been several waves of immigration since the early 17th century:

Date	Main countries of origin
1600–1790	England, Scotland, Ireland, the Netherlands, Germany
1790–1849	Ireland, Germany, Italy, Britain, France, Russia, China, Mexico, South America
1850–1930	Germany, Britain, Ireland, French Canada, Italy, Scandinavia, Poland, Eastern Europe (mainly Jews)
1930–present	the Philippines, Europe (post World War II, including refugees), Canada, Mexico, Korea, Hungary, Japan, Cuba, Vietnam, Latin America

Reasons for immigration

1st group of immigrants

- Members of religious groups that had broken away from the mainstream churches in their home country came to escape religious persecution (e.g. the Puritans from England).
- Colonies were settled to grow tobacco → immigrants were needed for this work.
- Land was cheap and economic conditions were better than at home.

2nd group of immigrants

- The Great Famine in Ireland drove the Irish to leave in their thousands.
- There was political instability in other parts of Europe, e.g. during and after the French Revolution.

- In 1849, gold was found in California, which started the gold rush → thousands of people travelled to the newly discovered gold fields in the hope of making their fortune.
- There were good chances of finding work in the US.

3rd group of immigrants

- People came to escape poverty in Europe.
- Between 1889 and 1924, approximately two million Jews emigrated to escape the pogroms in Eastern Europe.
- The Mexican Revolution from 1911–1929 resulted in more than one million refugees entering the USA.
- The economic boom in America in the second half of the 19th century encouraged many people to come and try their luck in the land of opportunity.

4th group of immigrants

- Most immigrants at this time came to escape war and oppression in their home countries.
- Jobs were plentiful after the end of the Second World War, when many women who had worked as part of the wartime effort went back to being housewives.
- From 1948, displaced people, especially from Europe, were allowed to emigrate to the States.
- People fleeing from Communist countries (e.g. Hungary, Cuba) were able to move to America.

SYMBOLS OF FREEDOM FOR NEW IMMIGRANTS

- **The Statue of Liberty:** new immigrants saw this symbol of freedom and independence when they sailed into New York.
- **Ellis Island:** new immigrants were taken here for medical checks and the examination of their documents before setting foot on mainland USA.

→ It was a symbol of hope: the end of a long journey and the beginning of a new life.

→ Some were kept on the island if they failed their medical test; they could even be sent back home if their documents were not correct.

The "melting pot" theory

The term "melting pot" has often been used to describe the integration process of immigrants in the US.

- The idea was that new immigrants would gradually give up their old lifestyles and help to **form a national identity**.
- The motto printed on American coins, **"e pluribus unum"** ("from many to one"), reflects this.
- This worked fairly well for the **first waves of immigrants**, up to the mid 19th century, as the **majority** of them were **white, northern European Protestants** who could identify with the ideas and values of the Puritan descendants and therefore assimilated well.
- From the mid 19th century, the immigrants came from a **far wider range of countries**, and as a result assimilation became more difficult.
- American citizens today do, to a certain extent, share a **national identity**, e.g. with regard to **language** (over 80 % of Americans speak only English at home) and **patriotic feelings**.
- However, a large number of people refer to their **ethnic origins** when asked to describe themselves → they are African American, or Irish American, rather than just "American".
- American social make-up today is often described as the **"salad bowl"**, **"mosaic"** or **"symphony"**.
- It consists of separate parts that make up a whole and work together, yet at the same time keeping their individual identities.

Abi Tipp

IMMIGRATION IN AMERICA

Make sure you know the significance of

- Manifest Destiny,
- the "melting pot" theory,
- the American Dream,

when talking about America as the land of opportunity. The terms will help you analyse immigration in the USA.

America's immigration policies

- Until the end of the 19th century, there were no restrictions on immigration to the States = there were plenty of jobs, and tickets for ships from Europe were relatively cheap.
- Settlers were encouraged to come, especially following Independence, to help establish the new nation.
- From the 20th century onwards, various laws and policies were introduced to control immigration → it became clear that the open door policy was not sustainable.
- The number of unskilled migrants admitted was reduced.
- Limits were set for the number of visas and green cards that could be issued every year.
- Today, there are different ways of getting a green card: through family already living in the States, through marriage to a US citizen, or through your employment.
- In addition to this, there is a "Diversity Visa Lottery". The idea is to allow a wider range of nationalities to emigrate to the US.
- Since it is a "lottery", applicants have to trust in luck to get a visa.

Undocumented immigrants

- There are around 11 million undocumented, or illegal, immigrants in the US, over half of which come from Mexico.
- Millions of US citizens and documented immigrants have undocumented family members → to get a family green card, they would first have to leave the country for 10 years. Most remain in the country illegally to stay with their families.
- A large number of undocumented people have children who were born in the US → this means the children are US citizens but their parents are not.
- Such people always live in fear of deportation → they can be arrested in their home or at their place of work.
- Some politicians believe that undocumented immigrants who have lived in the States for a significant period of time and who have made their life there should be granted residency.
- Many others, however disagree → during his election campaign, Donald Trump promised to crack down on illegal immigration and drastically cut the number of immigrants each year.
- He even pledged to build a wall along the border of the US and Mexico to keep people out.

The Civil Rights Movement

THE HISTORY OF BLACK PEOPLE IN THE USA

- integral part of the nation's social history
- has helped shape American society

The first Africans were brought to the US as slaves.

→ After the abolition of slavery, they faced decades of oppression.

→ Even the Civil Rights Movement could not completely eradicate this.

History of slavery and abolition in the US

- 1619–1808: Approximately 300,000 people were shipped from Africa to work as slaves in the USA.
- They lived mainly in the southern states and worked on the cotton, tobacco and sugar cane plantations. These crops were vital to the US economy; the plantation owners became very rich.
- After 1808, no more slaves were transported to the USA, but many were born in the country.
- 1833: The National Anti-Slavery Society was founded, although most of its supporters came from the northern states.
- 1865: Slavery was abolished after the American Civil War.
- 1868: The 14th Amendment of the Constitution gave black Americans the status of citizens.
- 1870: All male American citizens were given the right to vote, regardless of their race.

Freedom and discrimination

After the Civil War, African-Americans technically had the same rights as all other citizens. In practice, they suffered widespread discrimination and intimidation, particularly in the south:

- **Segregation** was practised in all walks of life. This was permitted by laws known as **"Jim Crow Laws"** (1880s): in a famous case brought to the Supreme Court in 1896, the judges ruled that segregation was not unconstitutional.
- Black people were **not allowed** to exercise their right **to vote**.

- They were **not given equal access to job opportunities**, so they remained poor and dependent.
- They were subjected to **acts of violence**, both in private and led by groups such as the **Ku Klux Klan**.
- From the 20th century onwards, many African-Americans **left the southern states** in hope of finding a better life in the more liberal northern and western states. However, even in these abolitionist areas **discrimination** was widespread.

THE CIVIL RIGHTS MOVEMENT

Key organisations in the movement:

- **National Association for the Advancement of Colored People =** founded 1909
- **Congress of Racial Equality =** founded 1942; organised peaceful demonstrations against segregation
- **Southern Christian Leadership Conference =** founded 1957 by Dr Martin Luther King, Jr.; used boycotts and peaceful demonstrations to end segregation
- **Black Muslims or Nation of Islam =** founded 1930; wanted a separate black state within the USA; Malcom X was a member
- **Black Panther Party =** founded 1966; used violence as a way to end discrimination

Key events in the Civil Rights Movement

- 1954: The NAACP won a famous court case, Brown v. Board of Education, which ruled that it was illegal to have separate schools for different races.
- 1955: Rosa Parks refused to give up her seat to white passengers on a public bus in Montgomery, Alabama → she was arrested and convicted for this. In protest, black people boycotted the buses for over a year in Montgomery until segregation on buses was lifted.
- 1961: Student volunteers took trips on interstate buses in the south to try and end segregation on public transport → the journeys were known as Freedom Rides.

- 1963: The March on Washington for Jobs and Freedom. Between 200,000 and 500,000 people from throughout the country staged a peaceful protest for civil rights. Martin Luther King, Jr., made his famous "I have a dream" speech, where he spoke of his hope that one day all Americans would be equal.
- 1965: The Voting Rights Act made it easier for minorities to register to vote.
- 1968: Martin Luther King, Jr. was assassinated.
- 1970 – 1976: To end segregation in schools, white children were taken by bus to schools in black areas, and vice versa.
- 1972: Laws were passed to encourage positive discrimination for ethnic minorities in the field of employment.
- 1984 and 1988: The Reverend Jesse Jackson was nominated as a presidential candidate for the Democratic Party: he inspired people from ethnic minorities to play an active role in politics.

African-Americans today

Positive aspects	Negative aspects
More black politicians, both at local and national level → Barack Obama was America's first African-American president, serving two terms in office from 2008 to 2016.	Many black people still live in deprived areas with high unemployment = it is easy to become involved in drug dealing or gangs.
More young African-Americans finish high school and college or university = better job prospects.	The high-school drop-out rate is still high among black students.
The movement "Black Lives Matter" was started in response to killings of young black people to raise awareness about police brutality against people of colour = a new attempt to fight the discrimination that still exists.	There have been many recent cases of young, unarmed black people being killed by white police officers → frequently, this has gone unpunished as the officers argued they were acting in self-defence.

Native Americans

PRE-COLONIAL INHABITANTS OF NORTH AMERICA

- There were probably at least 2 million Native Americans in North America before the first Europeans arrived.
- There were hundreds of tribes, each with their own language and culture.
- They believed they were part of the cycle of nature.
- They had no concept of property and land ownership → led to tension between the tribes and the new settlers

The Native Americans and the new settlers

- The first British settlers would probably have died in their new country without help from a friendly local tribe.
- Because the local Native Americans showed them how to survive, many more Europeans were able to settle in the country.
- The Europeans did not respect Native American beliefs and customs → some even tried to convert them to Christianity.
- The Native Americans had little resistance to European diseases such as smallpox or measles, and often died from them.
- Because many Native American tribes were nomadic, it was easier for the settlers to occupy their land.
- Many tribes were forced to live on reservations, which were often located in areas that were not good for farming, hunting and fishing → these poor conditions weakened the tribes further.
- There were wars between the Native Americans and the white settlers in which many natives were killed.
- The government made several treaties with the Native American tribes with regard to land ownership but often broke them.
- Many attempts were made to assimilate the Native Americans into white society by making it almost impossible for them to continue their traditional lifestyles → the long-term result was widespread poverty and depression among natives.
- Native Americans were not given American citizenship until 1924.
- In the 1970s that tribes were finally recognised as self-determining associations with the same rights as other ethnic groups.

Native Americans in the US today

- There are approximately 1.8 million registered tribal members.
- The federal government recognises 562 different tribal governments throughout the country.
- Native Americans still suffer from the long-term negative effects of European occupation, e.g. many suffer from mental health problems, alcoholism and heart disease.
- Many Native American governments get a large part of their income from casinos situated on their reservations. While some tribes feeling that getting revenue through gambling conflicts with their traditional culture, others use the money to build up a strong economy for themselves in order to improve their lives.

Crime and punishment in the US

VIOLENT CRIME

- The number of violent crimes, especially murder and gun crime, is higher than in other developed countries.
- African-Americans are far more likely to be victims of murder than people of other races → nearly half of all murder victims are black.
- Other social factors also play a role: young people and people from poor backgrounds are more likely to suffer from the effects of crime.

Why is there so much gun crime in the US?

- The Second Amendment to the Constitution states that citizens have the right to keep and bear arms.
- The National Rifle Association (NRA) is a powerful lobby group which campaigns against gun control based on the Second Amendment → it states that US citizens have the right to protect their families and their homes with a weapon.
- Around 40 % of Americans own a gun.
- However, most shootings in the home are not due to self-defence → a large percentage of them are accidents, e.g. if a child finds their parents' weapon and fires it.

Why is there so much gun crime in the US?

- In 2016, there were more than 38,000 gun-related deaths in the US.
- There were 263 mass shootings in the US in 2016.
- There have been nearly 300 school shootings since 2013. This statistic includes incidents where a gun was fired but nobody was injured.
- The school shooting with the highest death toll in recent years took place at Sandy Hook Elementary School in December 2012 → 21 six and seven-year olds were killed, along with six adults.

Response to gun crime

The response often seems illogical:

- The USA spends several billion dollars a year to protect itself against terrorist attacks, yet only a tiny number of people are killed by terrorism each year in comparison to the thousands killed by ordinary gun crime.
- Following the Sandy Hook shooting, the NRA reported a large increase in membership.
- Many people believe the best way to prevent school shootings is for teachers to have guns.
- Attempts (e.g. by President Obama) to pass laws that would tackle gun crime have been opposed in Congress.

The war on drugs

Drug and alcohol abuse are taken very seriously in the USA, with severe punishments for drug-related crimes. The government has tried various measures to prevent drug use, but without much success:

- The best-known historical example of an attempt to control drug use was **Prohibition** (1920 -1933), when alcohol was banned. However, **sales of alcohol** actually **increased** during this period, and a black market developed to meet the demand, as a result of which many people became extremely rich.
- In many US states, the **legal drinking** age is 21 rather than 16 or 18.
- Today the war on drugs tends to focus more on **narcotics**, especially the possession and sale of **marijuana**.
- **Prison sentences** are very common for drug-related crimes → pressure on the prison system
- Many companies now **test** their employees for **drug and alcohol usage** → members of staff who fail these tests can be fired.

Capital punishment

The USA is one of the 52 countries in the world that still retains and actively uses the death penalty as a means of punishment. The issue is extremely controversial, with emotional arguments on both sides. 1,466 people have been executed in the US since 1976.

Death penalty facts

- 35 of the 50 states have the death penalty on their statute books, although not all of them actively use this option.
- Texas executes the highest number of people.
- California has the largest number of people on death row but has not executed anyone since 2006.
- Due to the complicated appeal procedures, inmates often spend at least ten years on death row before they are executed.
- The most common method of execution today is the lethal injection, although, in the past, other methods such as the electric chair, gas chamber, hanging and firing squad have been used.
- Death row inmates are usually kept apart from other prisoners → they often spend up to 23 hours a day alone in their cells.
- Some state laws also allow the execution of juvenile offenders – people who were under 18 at the time they committed the crime.
- 156 death row inmates have been exonerated, i.e. found innocent and released, since 1973.

Arguments for the death penalty	Arguments against the death penalty
Anyone who deliberately kills another person does not deserve to live.	All human life is valuable, even that of killers, and the state does not have the right to take a life.
The families of victims are comforted by the fact that justice has been done.	Executing a killer will not bring their victim back to life; in fact, it means another family will lose a loved one.
The death penalty acts as a deterrent and makes society safer.	A large number of violent crimes are committed in rage on the spur of the moment, or under the influence of alcohol or drugs → the offender does not think about the consequences while committing the crime.

Arguments for the death penalty	Arguments against the death penalty
Life imprisonment without parole is not a good alternative, as laws can change and a convicted murderer could be released on parole at a later stage.	Life imprisonment without parole is a more suitable punishment and is cheaper than execution in the long run because of the very expensive legal processes required before someone can be put to death.
It may be possible that a few people that have been executed were, in fact, innocent – mistakes can be made. However, this is balanced out by the thousands of innocent victims killed by convicted murderers who were released early from prison. This would not have happened if those murderers had been executed.	The death penalty is not applied consistently. If the victim was white, a death sentence is more likely. Plus many offenders come from poor backgrounds and cannot afford a good lawyer → such people are also more likely to receive the death sentence. Some offenders are mentally ill and not entirely responsible for their actions.
If someone who takes a life is not executed, it implies that their victim's life was worthless, because their killer was not fully punished.	As long as there is a risk of even one innocent person being executed, the death penalty should be abolished.

The war on terrorism

9/11 AND ITS AFTERMATH

- On September 11 2001, Islamic extremists carried out four suicide attacks.
- They hijacked four planes: 2 were flown into the World Trade Center in New York City, one into the Pentagon and one crashed in the Pennsylvania countryside.
- Most victims were civilians or members of the emergency services.

Reaction

- The USA was left in a **state of shock** that it could be attacked on its own soil.
- There was a surge in displays of **patriotism**.
- Most of the world expressed **sympathy and support** for the USA.
- There were several **conspiracy theories**, e.g. that the US government had known about the attacks beforehand but did nothing to stop them.

US response to the attacks

- President Bush declared an international war on terrorism.
- Homeland Security and the US Patriot Act were introduced to prepare for, detect and prevent acts of terrorism.
- Military action was taken: 2001–2002 in Afghanistan → an attempt to defeat the Taliban and the Al Qaeda leader Osama bin Laden, who were thought have been behind the 9/11 attacks.
- 2003 –2011: the occupation of Iraq, to overthrow Saddam Hussein, who was also suspected of involvement and who was thought to have weapons of mass destruction.

Points of controversy

- Criticism of the infringements of civil liberties since the attacks → for example, the Patriot Act has given the authorities the right to secretly listen to phone calls and read e-mails.
- Since no evidence of weapons of mass destruction was found in Iraq the war there is considered unjustified by many.
- US troops were in Iraq for far too long → the government was under pressure to withdraw the troops after their presence there was clearly no longer necessary. President Obama did so in 2011.

TALKING POINTS: USA — Checkliste

Make sure you can answer the following questions on the USA!

- → Why is the American political system made up of three branches?
- → What are the most important aspects of the American Constitution?
- → What do the two main political parties stand for?
- → Who were the Puritans and why did they settle in America?
- → Describe the significance of the Puritan legacy.
- → What is the "American Dream" and is it still relevant today?
- → Describe the connection between "Manifest Destiny" and patriotism.
- → Why has America always been a popular destination for immigrants?
- → What were key events of the Civil Rights Movement?
- → Why is gun crime such a big problem in the USA?
- → What are the main arguments for and against the death penalty?

TALKING POINTS: GLOBALISATION

6

What is globalisation?

GLOBALISATION:

- the connection of various aspects of life such as the economy, business, environmental issues and culture
- not a new phenomenon: people have always been interested in discovering new places, adopting new ideas and spreading their own culture

Early globalisation

- The **Ancient Greeks** and **Romans** conquered large parts of the known world and brought their own culture to these places. E.g. the Romans built roads and introduced technologies such as central heating to Britain.
- The **Silk Road** was a collection of ancient trade routes that connected the east coast of China, Indonesia, India, Persia, Iran, eastern Africa and Europe. Goods such as silk, fabric, spices, perfumes and jewels were transported by land and sea routes.
- Religious and philosophical ideas were spread.
- The **Islamic Golden Age** (approx. 750 AD to 1257 AD) → Islamic civilisation spread through northern Africa, Arabia and western Asia. Ideas about art, philosophy, science, architecture and technology spread. The hajj (pilgrimage to Mecca) was a time when people came together to exchange ideas and trade goods, as well as pray.
- From the late 15th century, **European explorers** set out to discover the wider world. Most were from Portugal, Spain, Holland and Britain. They wanted to discover new trade routes. They brought back new foods, plants, animals and precious metals and established colonies e.g. to produce goods such as tobacco and cotton for export to the Old World. They established the slave trade between Africa and the Caribbean/America.

Modern globalisation

The **Industrial Revolution** was the start of modern globalisation goods were mass-produced for the first time. Britain became the world's first economic superpower in the 19th century. The USA took over this role due to abundance of cheap raw materials, natural resources and cheap labour.

The world as a "global village"

Positive aspects	Negative aspects
The world is connected through work, the economy, communications, international travel. → Distance no longer matters = reflects the closeness of village life	Many people do not like the ease of communication and sharing of personal information = comparable to village life where everyone knows your business
The easy, almost instant availability of products and communication makes the world seem much smaller.	The global availability of certain things means everything is the same everywhere → the things that make a culture special can be lost.

Globalisation and the economy

The **growth of international trade** has affected the economies of most countries in the world. There will, of course, always be winners and losers as a result of this: more often than not, the economies of the developed world are the winners, whereas developing countries, being more vulnerable to exploitation, frequently lose out.

Working conditions in developed countries

- Many developed countries have a minimum wage.
- Most allow workers to form and join trade unions.
- Workers can go on strike to protest about unfair conditions or pay.
- It is usually not possible to fire an employee without notice.
- There are industrial tribunals where employees can appeal if they feel they have been fired from their job for unfair or illegal reasons.
- Women usually have the right to paid maternity leave.

- Paternity leave for new fathers is becoming more common, as is parental leave, during which the parents can share the care of their young children at home.
- Conditions in offices and factories have to meet certain safety standards.
- Some form of unemployment benefit is normally available.
- Employees are entitled to paid holiday and sick leave.
- Companies in many countries have to pay health insurance contributions for their employees.

Working conditions in developing countries

- Employees are often expected to work long hours.
- They are paid low wages that are barely enough to live off.
- Workers often have to meet targets, i.e. they have to complete a certain amount of work within a given time. → If they do not manage this, they may have to work even longer hours, unpaid, until they have finished.
- The conditions inside the factories are often unhealthy and dangerous.
- Proper safety clothing and equipment is often not provided.
- Sick pay and unemployment benefit frequently do not exist.
- Trade unions are often forbidden, so workers have no official way of protesting about their conditions.
- Women often end up working in e.g. clothing factories because they are seen as easy to manipulate and less likely to complain about low pay.
- In extreme cases, teenagers or even children have to work in factories instead of going to school → often, they come from large families that urgently need the money.
- It is difficult for workers to negotiate better conditions for themselves → anyone seen as a trouble-maker can be fired and replaced.
- In some countries, such as Thailand or Bangladesh, people have been arrested for campaigning for better conditions for factory workers.
- Some companies may decide to move their factory to another area or another country if workers make too many demands → as a result, people desperate for a job accept the terrible working conditions to avoid losing their only source of income.

THESE CONDITIONS ARE A DIRECT CONSEQUENCE OF GLOBALISATION:

- The global economy enables companies to manufacture goods anywhere in the world.
- Companies want to increase their profits through lower production costs.
- Governments offer e.g. cheap rents and a cheap workforce to encourage foreign companies to set up business.
- The workers at the bottom of this chain lose out.

What can be done?

Global campaigns raise awareness about the origins of the products we buy. Groups such as the Clean Clothes Campaign lobby companies and governments to improve conditions and stop exploitation. People need to know the true cost of their cheap T-shirt from Vietnam.

One solution: “fair trade” products

- Fair trade products are ones that guarantee higher prices, good working conditions, local sustainability and trade on fair terms for workers and farmers in developing countries.
- Companies that buy fair trade goods agree to pay no less than the market price.
- Farmers working for fair trade organisations are in control of their working conditions. → They are paid sustainable prices for their products, so they can cover their costs and actually live off the money they earn.
- Fair trade associations make money available for investment in social, environmental and economic development projects.
- Some producers need money before they can start producing their goods: for example, farmers may need to buy fertilizers or seeds before they can begin growing. → Fair trade organisations make it possible for them to get the money they need, which they can then repay when they start earning from the sale of their products.
- Fair trade allows long-term trading partnerships to be established in which all parties have a say in the way business is done.

One solution: "fair trade" products

- Fair trade is a positive effect of globalisation: people who would not otherwise have been able to make a living in the global marketplace are able to sell their products internationally.
- The market for fair trade goods is growing. → People like to feel good about what they are buying.
- All major supermarkets now carry a range of ethically sourced products.
- Many food outlets used fair trade ingredients.

Migration of workers

Globalisation has increased the mobility of workers.

- That is not a new phenomenon → large numbers of people migrated to the USA in search of the **American Dream**.
- Canada and Australia are also popular destinations for Europeans → opportunities in the **New World.**

Today, moving abroad for work can be both easier and more difficult than in the past, depending on the circumstances.

Positive aspects	Negative aspects
EU citizens have the right to live and work in other member countries without a work permit or visa.	Many people are driven to look for work in another country because there are no jobs in their homeland. → They usually have to look for unskilled work, e.g. because they do not speak the language.
The internet makes it easy to search and apply for jobs throughout the world.	It is often difficult to find unskilled jobs in developed countries, due to technological developments that have enabled companies to cut back on workers.
Some countries have a lack of skilled workers in certain fields and offer highly qualified professionals from abroad incentives to come and work there.	Seasonal work, such as fruit picking, is often done by migrant workers → they are paid a lower wage than average.

Positive aspects	Negative aspects
Workers can experience life in another culture.	Some people, desperate for a better life, go to dangerous lengths to emigrate to a country where they think they will have a better chance of finding work. For example, people from Africa undertake the perilous journey by boat across the Mediterranean Sea to southern Europe. Frequently, the boats – which are often unsuitable for a journey of this kind – run into difficulties when the sea turns rough. Many of the potential immigrants never make it, but drown or die in terrible conditions on the overcrowded boat.

THE “BRAIN DRAIN”

- The global economy makes it easier and more attractive for highly qualified professionals to work abroad. However, this becomes a problem when large numbers of highly skilled workers leave:
- When there are not enough workers with the right skills, the country cannot remain competitive.
- This “brain power” is “drained away” and disappears.
- Such people often leave countries with weak economies (such as Greece) to a better life. → However, these are exactly the people needed to help rebuild the economy.
- If highly qualified people enter a country as a refugee or asylum seeker, they are often not allowed to practise their profession and are forced to do jobs far below their skill level. → The host country does not make use of their professional skills = “brain waste”.

Globalisation and the environment

Globalisation has a significant effect on the ecology of our planet:

- **Travel** is cheaper and easier than ever.
- People want to choose from a **wide range of food and products**, not just what is available locally.
- The infrastructure necessary to make this happen **damages our planet.**
- However, people are starting to **rethink their behaviour** and try to **reverse** some of the negative effect on the environment.

A planet on the move

- Large numbers of people **fly regularly.**
- Many people in developed countries **own a car.**
- We use more and more **fossil fuels** to keep us mobile.
- Planes and cars add to **pollution levels**, contributing to **global warming.**

Flying

- Budget airlines encourage short trips both for business and pleasure; more people fly long distances to exotic locations.
- Although planes now have new technologies that allow them to use fuel more efficiently, and biofuels have been developed for aircraft use, the problem of pollution remains because of the increase in passenger numbers and freight transported by air.
- As the volume of air travel continues to rise, many airports feel the need to expand, for example by building an additional runway, to cope with the higher number of flights.
- This has an additional impact on the environment → part of the countryside has to be destroyed to build the runway, affecting the natural habitats of animals and plants in the area.
- It also means more noise and pollution for people living near the airport.
- Whenever an airport proposes expansion, there are strong protests from local residents and environmental groups. Those responsible for giving the go-ahead, for example politicians, will always weigh up the environmental issues against the economic benefits and often decide in favour of expansion for this reason.

- It seems unlikely that flying will become less popular any time soon. → There are, however, some things that can be done to reduce the need for flying, particularly for work reasons:
  → make more use of video conferencing technology so that meetings can take place remotely, rather than in person,
  → scrap frequent flyer programmes so that people have less incentive to fly often,
  → encourage people to go on holiday in their home country and travel there by train.
- However, it would be surprising if such measures had a significant effect on the number of people travelling by plane.
- Moreover, the amount of international freight being transported by air is unlikely to decrease, as it is so much faster than the alternative methods of shipping.

Cars

- For many people in the western world, life without a car would be unimaginable.
- Carbon dioxide emissions from car exhaust fumes have added considerably to the amount of air pollution, which in its turn contributes to the greenhouse effect, and therefore to global warming.
- In some places, particularly in rural areas, it is difficult to live without a car due to a lack of public transport → bus and train services are often infrequent or non-existent, leaving residents with no choice but to drive everywhere.
- Car manufacturers have recognised the importance of producing vehicles that are more energy-efficient and can run on cleaner fuels: there are now a large number of hybrid and electric cars.
- To reduce pollution, many cities in Germany have environmental green zones → only cars with a low emission value and marked with a green badge can drive there.

GLOBAL WARMING

- The average temperature of our planet is rising.
- This has happened in the past, following ice ages, but slowly.
- Today, human activities are contributing to the higher temperatures, making them rise much faster than they should.
- Climate change also has natural causes, such as the flow of water in the oceans, changes in solar radiation that reach the Earth, or volcanic eruptions.
- This is why some people do not believe climate change is caused by human behaviour. They argue that temperatures will rise anyway and will probably fall again at some point in the future.
- However, there is evidence that human activities are the most significant factor in global warming today.
- It may already be too late to undo most of the damage.

Human activities contributing to global warming

- Burning fossil fuels (e.g. for vehicles and manufacturing) has increased the amount of greenhouse gases in the atmosphere, which in turn make temperatures rise.
- Making significant changes to the surface of the planet, e.g. by cutting down large areas of forest.

→ For example, the rainforests of Brazil are far smaller now compared to a few decades ago, as they have been cut down to make way for farmland or to provide wood for commercial activities.

- Trees play an important role in absorbing the greenhouse gas CO_2. → Fewer trees means more of this gas can escape into the atmosphere.
- The use of aerosols and appliances containing CFC gases, such as fridges. → These gases considerably damage the ozone layer, which is needed to protect the planet from dangerous rays from the sun.

Consequences of global warming

- A considerable amount of the world's ice will melt (e.g. the ice caps and the north and south poles, the Greenland and Antarctic ice sheets), causing sea levels to rise.
- This in turn will cause more flooding in lowland areas.

- Some parts of the globe will become far hotter, especially in the northern hemisphere. → There will be more heat waves, and rainfall is likely to become far heavier than it is now, again leading to an increase in flooding.
- People living in coastal areas will be at greater risk from flooding.
- The rising sea levels will particularly threaten small islands, e.g. the Maldives, making it difficult or impossible for people to continue to live there.
- The amount of clean water available will be reduced, which in turn will have a negative effect on the health of many people.
- There will be a reduction in the amount of crops that can be grown, particularly in developing countries such as India.
- At the same time, the population in these countries is expected to rise dramatically.

→ likely result = an increase in diseases connected to malnutrition, as well as more famines

What can we do to reduce the effects of global warming?

- Make more efficient use of **alternative energy sources.**
- Reduce the amount of **energy** we use, e.g. by switching off electrical appliances that are not in use.
- **Use our cars less** → instead, take public transport, go by bike or carpool, at least some of the time.
- **Reforestation**: trees can be planted to replace those that have been cut down → **buy paper products** made from wood pulp that is certified as coming from a sustainable forest.
- **Recycle waste** and choose **recycled** products.
- Avoid buying products that come with a **large amount of packaging.**
- Buy **energy-efficient** appliances, e.g. washing machines, that use less water.
- **Turn down the heating** in our homes by a couple of degrees.
- **New buildings** can be designed to be **energy-efficient**, using **renewable energy sources** for heating and electricity.
- More goods could be **transported by rail** rather than by air or road.
- **Public transport** can be made more attractive to use → buses can run on **biofuel** or **electricity**.
- **Town planners** can make urban development more energy-efficient, which in turn provides a **better quality of life** for the citizens (for

example by **reducing pollution**). This can be achieved, among other things, by

- including plenty of **parks** and **green spaces,**
- planning the location of e.g. shops in residential areas, so there is **no need to travel long distances** to reach them or to go by car,
- improve **public transport** infrastructure,
- make travelling by car to the city centre less attractive by making **parking expensive,**
- provide **safe cycle paths,**
- make **walking more pleasant** (e.g. with wider pavements).

What can governments do about global warming?

To really stop global warming, changes are needed on a **national** and **international** level. All **governments** have a **responsibility** to tackle the problem, e.g. by signing – and **following** – agreements on measures to be taken. The **Kyoto Protocol** is one example of this.

The Kyoto Protocol

- It came into effect in February 2005.
- It was an agreement to reduce greenhouse gas emissions by 5.2 % each year by 2012.
- It was signed and ratified by 192 states → the nations that did not ratify it were the USA, Afghanistan and Sudan.
- The USA refused to ratify it because it claimed that scientific evidence of the effects of greenhouse gases was not convincing; they were also afraid of damaging the US economy.
- Unfortunately, many countries failed to meet their agreed targets → they can be fined, but cannot be forced to make the necessary changes.
- In the USA in particular, large businesses put pressure on the government not to pass laws that will force them to change the way they work, especially if this will cost them more.
- Some countries, e.g. India and China, did not have to agree to national limits when they signed the protocol, as they were not among the world's largest greenhouse gas emitters at that time.
- However, since then, a surge in industrialisation in China means it now produces the most greenhouse gases in the world, pushing the USA into second place.

The Kyoto Protocol

- Since the Kyoto Protocol, there have been more attempts to reach international agreements on climate change, but it remains a difficult problem:
  - → 2009: the Copenhagen Accord agreed to try and limit global warming, but acknowledged that developing countries would need more time and financial support to meet these goals.
  - → 2014: during climate talks in Paris, the USA and others said they would not sign an agreement to reduce CO_2 emissions.
  - → 2015: the Paris Agreement pledged to slow climate change. → By November 2017, 194 states and the European Union had signed the agreement; 173 of them, including the USA, China and India, had ratified it.
  - → However, in 2017, the American government under President Trump gave notice that the country was going to withdraw from the Paris Agreement.

RENEWABLE ENERGY SOURCES

- **Wind power:** "Wind farms" are placed in areas with high, constant wind speeds, e.g. offshore → turbines create energy that is turned into electricity.
- **Solar power:** The sun's rays are collected in solar panels → can also be used for individual buildings and private homes to provide heat and hot water.
- **Hydropower:** The energy in flowing water, usually in rivers, is used to make electricity.
- **Biomass:** Energy is created by burning wood and other organic material. → The plants absorb the sun's energy while growing, which is released when they are burnt.
- **Biofuels:** come from biomass and can be solid, liquid or gas. Example: bioethanol, which can be used to power cars, is a type of alcohol made from sugar and starch crops (sugarcane, wheat, corn).
- **Geothermal energy:** The heat comes from beneath the Earth's surface (the same energy that heats natural hot springs) can be used to generate electricity.

The use of renewable energy can make a considerable difference to life in developing countries:

- Particularly in rural areas, it is not possible for households to be connected to an electricity supply.
- However, small solar panels can be installed in villages, providing lighting and heat for cooking at half the price of kerosene, which was commonly the only option in such places.
- There are also other positive effects: if power is available, people are able to start up a business and earn money.
- In addition to this, options for education improve, as schools can be provided with electricity.

Food: global versus local

People nowadays think more carefully about where their food comes from:

- In the past, all food was locally grown, often by individual families for their own needs.
- Today, both exotic and "ordinary" food is available throughout the world and throughout the year.
- People love having a wide choice of products to buy at their local supermarket.

Food miles

- This term refers to the distance the food has to travel from the place it was grown to the consumer.
- The method of transportation is a factor in the environmental impact of food miles → have the goods travelled a short distance by road or been flown in from the other side of the world?
- There are campaigns that encourage consumers to buy locally grown food, seasonal fruit and vegetables, and meat products from local sources.
- This seems to make good sense:

→ Fruit and vegetables are healthier if they are in season and have not travelled thousands of miles.
→ Buying local meat helps to ensure the animals have not been transported live, under cruel conditions.
→ Buying local products helps to support local businesses and maintain local jobs rather than large, anonymous companies.
→ However, the situation is not as clear-cut as it may seem:
→ More greenhouse gases are released during food cultivation and production than through transportation of the products.

Food miles

- → A lot depends on the conditions in which the animals are kept: it is more energy-efficient to keep animals that can eat fresh grass from the field all year round than those that need additional food.
- → We should therefore consider how food is produced, and not only how far it has travelled.

Global organisations

THE UNITED NATIONS

- founded in October 1945 after World War II
- 51 formed the UN as a replacement for the League of Nations.
- Its headquarters are in New York City.
- It has 193 member states.
- The International Court of Justice, also part of the UN, is located in The Hague in the Netherlands. → People, e.g. heads of state, accused of humanitarian crimes are tried there.
- Organisations closely linked to the UN include UNICEF and refugee programmes such as UNHCR.

The UN has four main aims:

- to **maintain peace and security** throughout the world,
- to **develop relations** among nations,
- to **encourage cooperation** between nations to solve economic, social, cultural or humanitarian problems,
- to provide a forum for **countries to come together** in an attempt to meet the UN's purposes.

International peacekeeping

- Peacekeeping and peace building are two of the UN's most important functions.
- It aims to maintain peace in the long-term once it has been established, and encourage mediation to solve conflicts:

International peacekeeping

- UN peacekeepers go to countries and regions that have previously been at conflict to help with the peace process.
- This includes overseeing elections, providing funds to help rebuild the country or region, and supporting military withdrawal post-war.
- UN peacekeepers are often soldiers, but can also be police officers or civilians.
- The UN does not have its own army, so soldiers acting on behalf of the UN are still part of their own country's army.
- As an international peacekeeping organisation, the UN is able to remain neutral in conflict regions.
- There are currently 15 active UN peacekeeping missions, e.g. in Mali and Libya.

Global communication: the role of the internet

The internet is the global phenomenon that has affected our everyday lives the most dramatically in recent years:

- It is **deeply integrated** in our lives, even in ordinary activities.
- It is **accessible nearly everywhere** in the world.
- We can go online **anywhere** and at **any time**.

Abi Tipp

THE INTERNET – PROS AND CONS

You may be asked to give your opinion about pros and cons of the internet as a global phenomenon.

- You will find many arguments for and against the various aspects of the internet.
- Choose the most relevant.
- You can agree or disagree, as long as you have arguments to back up the point you are making.

Availability of information

Pros	Cons
The internet contains information on every subject that exists. → Search engines help us find the information we want.	There are websites on subjects that many people do not want to see, e.g. Neo-Nazi sites → it can be difficult for parents to completely control what their children see.
Users can keep up-to-date with world affairs and other news as it happens.	Danger of "fake news" → it is important to check the facts behind a story, especially if it seems unusual or shocking.
The internet has become a library that is accessible to everybody → online dictionaries and encyclopaedias make it easy to look things up.	There is no guarantee that all the information found online is accurate → it is important to check more than one source when doing research.
The internet helps people because they can find answers to all kinds of problems, saving time and money → e.g. by looking up how to solve a computer problem.	Some things are still difficult to do without expert knowledge → online videos can encourage people e.g. to attempt repairs that they are not qualified to do. They can hurt themselves or damage their appliance.
People search for advice on medical problems → they look for reassurance about symptoms they have.	It can be dangerous to work out a medical diagnosis for yourself instead of going to a doctor → not all information online is accurate.

The online community – pros

- Many people enjoy being part of an online community where they can talk about a shared interest.
- Some communities are like a support group, for example for people suffering from a particular medical condition.
- Unlike "real-life" support groups, online forums are available at all times → members have someone to talk to whenever they need it.

- They can share their experiences with a much wider range of people and get faster answers to their questions.
- Some people find it helpful to talk to others who understand their situation while remaining anonymous.

The online community – cons

- Some people come to rely too much on advice given in forums rather than consulting a professional.
- We do not know who the other people in the forum are → anonymity can be dangerous.

The world of work - pros	The world of work - cons
The internet has revolutionised the way we work → for many jobs, it is no longer necessary to sit in an office all day every day, as the work can be done from another location.	Working life has become more stressful → technologies such as e-mail and mobile phones mean that employees are always available, even outside office hours or when on holiday
It is easy for professionals working in a particular field to exchange knowledge and ideas without having to travel.	Some companies, for example, expect e-mails to be answered straight away, increasing pressure on workers.

The role of bloggers – pros

- The internet is not a passive medium, but is a resource that everyone can contribute to. Blogging is a common way of doing this.
- While some blogs are merely personal, an online diary of their author's thoughts, others reach a far wider audience, with hundreds of thousands of clicks per day.
- Political bloggers can provide important information and comment on current situations.
- The internet makes it easier for people to practice freedom of speech.

The role of bloggers – cons

- In countries with repressive regimes, such as China or Iran, blogging is often seen as a real threat to the state and is subject to censorship.
- Governments are afraid that certain information will become known in the wider world, or that their citizens might find out the truth about certain situations through the internet.
- In extreme cases, bloggers may even be arrested and imprisoned for expressing their views.

Social media – more pros than cons?

1	Social media connects people → easy way to communicate, share news and photos.
2	Users can join groups connected to their interests and hobbies.
3	Sites like Facebook and Twitter are good for promoting events and causes → a large number of people can be reached quickly.
4	People can use professional networking sites to connect with others in their field and get a new job.
5	Social media can play a political role. During the "Arab Spring" of 2011, civil unrest that had started in Tunisia and Egypt spread throughout North Africa and the Middle East as people took to the streets to protest against their governments. The success of these protests is partly due to the use of Facebook and Twitter to coordinate events and mobilise large numbers of people. Afterwards, people uploaded videos they had taken at the protests so that the rest of the world could see what was going on, making it impossible for the governments to lie about it.
6	The example of the Arab Spring shows that social media can be a very powerful tool in making sure the truth is told, and that corruption and human rights violations are made public.

1	On the downside: it is easy to be anonymous on the internet and for people to disguise who they really are → it is essential to consider what kind of personal details can be viewed by the general public and to have strong security settings.
2	Once something has been posted online, it can be difficult to make it disappear again.
3	There are now employers who check up on the social media pages of job applicants. Depending on what they find there, they may decide not to offer the person a job.

4	People often have far less personal contact with their friends, spending more time chatting to them digitally than face to face.
5	The problem of cyberbullying is connected to social media sites.

CYBERBULLYING

- The anonymity of the internet makes it easy for people to tease or even threaten others.
- Comments posted online are seen, more or less instantly, by hundreds of other people.
- They may in turn add their own comments or forward the original post to others, spreading the message further.
- The victim of the bullying cannot do much to stop this.
- People who comment on such posts do not always consider that they are helping to bully someone. They may see it as a joke.
- However, victims often suffer from anxiety or depression. In extreme cases, they may be driven to suicide.

TALKING POINTS: GLOBALISATION

Checkliste

Make sure you can answer the following questions about globalisation!

→ What is meant by the term “global village”?

→ What effects do globalisation have on employment in developing countries?

→ What can be done to limit the exploitation of workers in developing countries?

→ What kinds of human activities contribute to global warming and what can we do about this?

→ What are some of the advantages and disadvantages of living in the internet age?

7

TALKING POINTS: SCIENCE AND ETHICS

Genetic engineering

What are genes?

Our genes make us what we are:

- They are the **features**, or **traits**, that we inherit from our ancestors, e.g. our **hair or eye colour**.
- This applies to **all living organisms**, not just human beings.

Certain diseases are also passed down through the generations:

- Scientists can use **genetics** to work out the likelihood of a child developing some diseases.
- This kind of research can help people decide whether they should have children or not.
- It may be possible to **prevent some diseases** by manipulating an embryo's genes.
- This raises a **question of ethics**.

How genes work

- DNA is the molecule in our bodies that carries genetic information.
- Our DNA makes copies of itself and is passed on to our descendants.
- Genes work by providing information that allows an organism to build or do something, e.g. to create blue eyes → it is as if they write instructions for our cells.
- A **genome** is the complete set of genes in an organism.
- Every time a cell in our bodies divides to make two new cells, the genes it contains are copied, so the genes are continuously passed on.

GENETIC ENGINEERING

- Scientists have discovered that it is possible to change, or "engineer", genes in order to modify an organism's DNA.
- This can be used e.g. for farming, to increase the amount of crops grown.
- Humans can be treated with gene therapy if they suffer from certain genetic disorders → the defective gene can be replaced.

The development of genetic engineering

- Long ago, it was observed that, for example, members of the same family looked similar.
- The first scientific studies of this phenomenon took place in the mid 19th century:

→ 1859: Charles Darwin developed his theory of evolution, which showed how organisms gradually change over time, adapting to changes in the world around them.

→ 1865: Gregor Mendel discovered how traits are passed on from one generation to the next while experimenting with pea plants.

→ 1905: William Bateson coined the term "genetics" → it comes from the Greek word "genno" meaning "give birth".

→ 1944: Experiments by Oswald Avery and colleagues proved that DNA is responsible for inheritance.

→ 1953: James Watson and Francis Crick discovered DNA at the University of Cambridge.

→ 1972: The first gene sequence was decoded.

→ 1978: Synthetic human insulin was products for the first time. Insulin was the first human protein to be manufactured using biotechnology.

→ 1980s: Scientists began experimenting with human genes.

→ 1996: An animal was successfully cloned for the first time → Dolly the sheep

What can knowledge of the human genome be used for?

- improving genetic testing
- preventative medicine → it will be easier to accurately predict if someone will develop certain illnesses in the future and take steps to prevent it.

- assessing the chances of someone developing a particular disease
- developing new gene therapies
- creating personalised medicines to treat individual people for individual conditions
- improving DNA testing which can be used e.g. in forensic medicine to solve crimes
- working towards cloning human organs that can be used for organ transplants

CLONING

- Thanks to genetic research, scientists know how to clone organisms.
- It is difficult to make a genetic copy of an animal → the first successful clone of a mammal was Dolly the sheep.
- Other types of mammals have been successfully cloned since then.

Is animal cloning a good or a bad thing?

Arguments for cloning	Arguments against cloning
The clones are genetically identical so they will have the required characteristics, e.g. cows that produce a lot of milk can be cloned to make a dairy farm more productive.	If one clone is affected by a disease or changes in the environment, all of the others will be affected too.
It may be possible to save species from extinction through cloning, or even bring extinct species back to life.	Cloning leads to less variation, and limits the opportunities for creating new varieties in the future. A lack of variation within a species that can lead to extinction.

Another form of cloning:

- Attempts have been made to **grow human organs on animals** such as pigs.
- These organs could then be **transplanted** into people who need a new one.

It is not currently possible to say whether this will be a real option at some time in the future.

STEM CELL RESEARCH

- Embryos have a special type of cell called **stem cells**.
- These cells can grow into any type of cell in the body → they are not specialised to become e.g. an organ, as most cells are.
- They can be taken out of human embryos that are a few days old and used for medical purposes, e.g.
- making new brain cells for people with Parkinson's disease,
  → repairing a person's damaged immune system,
- making replacement heart valves,
- rebuilding bones.

Therapeutic cloning – an ethical dilemma

- It may be possible to clone a person's cells to produce an embryo with their own genes.
- Stem cells could be taken from this embryo and used to develop the cells needed to treat that person's medical condition.
- Advantage = The body would not reject its own cells.
- Problem = The ethics of creating an embryo for this purpose.

Uses of genetic engineering

Plants can be genetically modified

- to be resistant to pesticides,
- so that they will not be eaten by pests,
- to be more resistant to certain environmental conditions,
- to make them more nutritious (e.g. by adding vitamins),
- so that they yield more within a smaller space,
- to last longer before going bad → longer shelf life in shops.

Genetically modified (GM) crops

Advantages	Disadvantages
The land is used more efficiently.	The genes could mutate in ways that are not good for the plants.
The yield of the individual plants is greater.	GM crops do not produce seeds, so the farmer has to buy new ones every time a new crop is to be planted.

Advantages	Disadvantages
Farming with certain GM crops is less damaging to the land → no need for pesticides or fertilizer; the ground does not have to be ploughed up.	Can have a negative effect on birds and insects that eat the plants → introducing something unnatural to the ecosystem.
The quality of the food can be improved.	Through eating crops that have been made resistant to antibiotics, we can also become resistant, leaving us more vulnerable to certain diseases.
The food can be made healthier.	We do not know what the long-term effects of GM crops in the food chain will be.
The food does not go bad so quickly → better e.g. for supermarkets if fruit/vegetables do not have to be thrown away at the end of the day.	Farmers have to depend on large companies to get the seeds they need → they cannot farm sustainably.

"Designer babies"

- Embryos can already be **modified** to prevent the child from developing certain diseases.
- Some scientists envision creating a **"super human"** through genetics. = a child that is as perfect as possible.
- Parents could also be given the option of choosing their child's physical features → i.e. **create a "designer baby".**

Abi Tipp

LITERATURE AND FACT

- Many writers have imagined what the world might be like if we could eradicate disease or create a world of "super humans".
- One well-known example is Aldous Huxley's "Brave New World", which describes a society where embryos are bred in laboratories and workers are cloned.
- When writing essays on your set books, it is interesting to compare fact with fiction using real-life examples.

The ethics of genetic engineering

Some people regard genetic engineering as scientific progress, a way to improve life on earth. Others feel we should not "play God" and change nature to suit our purposes. But how far is "too far" along this road?

Genetic engineering: arguments in favour	Ethical dilemmas
There is nothing wrong with the genetic modification of embryos: parents have the right to choose the physical features of their children.	The technology is not safe and may never be completely safe.
Parents should make sure their children have the best possible life. → This includes ensuring they will not have to suffer from genetic diseases.	Perfect health does not guarantee a good life. → There are many outside factors too.
The human species will become stronger and better able to survive in the future if our genes are better.	If we create a race of "super humans", they may feel it is their right to mistreat ordinary people. → possible discrimination of disabled people
Parents should have the right to choose the gender of their child.	We already have the example of societies in the world that prefer boys to girls, and encourage women to abort female foetuses. → creates an imbalance in society and, often, a large surplus of males who cannot find a female partner.
The use of stem cells for medical research helps people who are in a desperate situation → If they are lucky, a cure will be found.	Embryos are living creatures and using them for research in this way is murder.

TALKING POINTS: SCIENCE AND ETHICS — Checkliste

Make sure you can answer the following questions!

- → What can genetic engineering be used for?
- → What are the advantages and disadvantages of animal cloning?
- → Why are some people against stem cell research?
- → What is meant by a "designer baby" and what ethical problems does this idea create?
- → Describe some arguments for and against genetic engineering.

8

DIE SPRACHLICHE LEISTUNG IM ABITUR

WIE STRUKTURIERT MAN EINEN TEXT?

- Ihre Texte sollten flüssig lesbar und logisch nachvollziehbar sein.
- Nützlich sind dazu Redemittel, die dabei helfen, Ihre Sätze zu verbinden. Eine gute Auswahl finden Sie in den folgenden Tabellen.
- Die ausgewählte Begriffe müssen zum Sprachregister des jeweiligen Textes passen.

Listing facts, ideas and reasons	Aufzählen von Fakten, Ideen und Begründungen
firstly, ... secondly, ... thirdly	erstens, ... zweitens, ... drittens, ...
furthermore	zudem, weiterhin
in addition to	zusätzlich
as well as	sowie
finally	schließlich
last but not least	zu guter Letzt, schließlich doch noch

Stating opposites/contrast	Gegensatz/Kontrast
yet	dennoch, trotzdem
however	jedoch
on the other hand	andererseits
on the contrary	im Gegensatz, hingegen
in spite of/despite	trotz, trotzdem
although	obwohl

Stating conditions	Bedingungen nennen
if	falls, wenn
unless	außer, falls nicht
provided that	insofern

Stating consequences	Folgen nennen
because	weil
since	da
consequently	infolgedessen
as a result	dadurch
therefore	daher, deshalb
accordingly	dementsprechend, demzufolge

Making comparisons	Vergleiche anstellen
in comparison with	im Vergleich zu
likewise	ebenfalls, ebenso
similarly	gleichermaßen, ähnlich
As ... as	So ... wie

Abi Tipp

ACHTUNG: GRAMMATIK!

- Sie sollen unbedingt darauf achten, dass Sie die Redemittel grammatikalisch korrekt verwendet haben.
- Notieren Sie deshalb die Redemittel jeweils mit einem Beispielsatz in Ihr Vokalbelheft, damit der Kontext klar ist.

Ein logischer Aufbau ist für gute Texte unabdingbar. Die folgenden Redemittel werden Ihnen dabei helfen.

Introducing a topic	Ein Thema einführen
It has often been said ...	Es wurde schon oft gesagt ...
As a general statement ...	Als grundsätzliche Aussage ...
Many people would agree that ...	Viele Menschen würden zustimmen, dass ...

Expressing facts	Fakten ausdrücken
The fact is that ...	Es ist Fakt, dass ...
It cannot be denied that ...	Es kann nicht verleugnet, dass ...
It is obvious that ...	Es ist offensichtlich, dass ...

Speculating	Vermutungen ausdrücken
It may be the case ...	Eventuell ...
Apparently ...	Scheinbar ...
It seems highly likely that ...	Höchstwahrscheinlich ...

Expressing agreement or disagreement	Zustimmung oder Ablehnung ausdrücken
This statement is very convincing.	Diese Aussage ist sehr überzeugend.
It is only partly true that ...	Es stimmt nur teilweise, dass ...
I do not agree with ...	Ich stimme nicht mit ... zu
This statement entirely contradicts ...	Diese Aussage steht in völligem Widerspruch zu ...

Conclusion and expressing your opinion	Schlussfolgerung und die eigene Meinung ausdrücken
As a consequence ...	Demzufolge ...
As a result ...	Infolgedessen ...
In my opinion ...	Meiner Meinung nach ...
I come to the conclusion that ...	Ich komme zu dem Schluss, dass ..
From my point of view ...	Von meinem Standpunkt aus betrachtet ...

Verwenden Sie unterschiedliche grammatikalische Strukturen, wechseln Sie etwa zwischen aktiv und passiv. Vermeiden Sie unnötige Wortwiederholungen. Nutzen Sie Synonyme oder Umschreibungen.

Frequently overused words	Alternatives
to say	to affirm; to announce; to claim; to declare; to express; to refer to; to remark; to state; to suggest
to think	to believe; to consider; to suppose
because	as; since
because of	on account of; as a consequence; due to; thanks to

DIE SPRACHLICHE LEISTUNG IM ABITUR — Checkliste

- → Legen Sie Wert auf Redemittel, die Ihnen dabei helfen, flüssige Texte zu schreiben.
- → Achten Sie auf das Sprachregister: Manche Redemittel sind eher für formelle Texte geeignet, andere dagegen sind für informelle Texte angemessener.
- → Achten Sie auf grammatikalisch korrekte Verwendung.
- → Achten Sie zudem darauf, dass Ihre Sprache abwechslungsreich sein sollte.

DIE INTERPRETATION LITERARISCHER TEXTE

9

Lyrik *(poetry)*

DIE SPRACHE UNTER DIE LUPE NEHMEN

Bei der Analyse eines Gedichts ist es besonders wichtig, darauf zu achten, wie die Sprache verwendet wird:

- Wie klingen die Wörter?
- Haben sie einen bestimmten Rhythmus?
- Welchen Rhythmus kann man in den Versen des Gedichts erkennen?
- Welche Wörter hat der Dichter ausgesucht, um seine Ideen auszudrücken?
- Wie sind die Verse strukturiert?
- Welche Stilmittel werden verwendet?

Das lyrische Ich

Wer „spricht" in dem Gedicht? Es gibt zwei Arten des lyrischen Ichs *(speaker)*:

- das **explizite lyrisches Ich** *(explicit speaker)*
  → Verwendung von *I, my, mine, me*
- das **implizierte lyrische Ich** *(implicit speaker)*
  → Dieses Ich tritt im Gedicht nicht direkt auf, es ist nur angedeutet, man kann auch sagen, es ist versteckt: Der Leser muss es erst entdecken.

Abi Tipp

LYRISCHES ICH UND DER AUTOR

Das lyrische Ich eines Gedichts ist **nicht** identisch mit dem Ich des Dichters. Das lyrische Ich ist ein (fiktiver) Charakter, den der Autor (ein reales Ich) erschaffen hat. Inwieweit das lyrische Ich im Gedicht beispielsweise Meinungen/Einstellungen/Gefühle des Autors ausdrückt, kann natürlich diskutiert werden.

Leitfragen zum lyrischen Ich

- Wer ist das lyrische Ich?
- Wen will das lyrische Ich ansprechen?
- Was macht das lyrische Ich?
  - → Beobachtet es etwas/jemand?
  - → Beschreibt es eine Situation?
  - → Erzählt es eine Geschichte?
  - → Erklärt es dem Leser etwas?
  - → Argumentiert es für oder gegen etwas?
  - → Hat es eine feststellbare Einstellung zu angesprochenen Themen?

Weitere Leitfragen

- Hat das Gedicht eine einfache oder komplexe Struktur?
- Verwendet der Dichter Reime? Welches Reimschema liegt vor?
- Welche Stilmittel werden im Gedicht verwendetet?
- In welchem Bezug steht der Titel zum Inhalt des Gedichts?

Satzbau

Die **Syntax** in Gedichten unterscheidet sich oft von dem in Prosatexten üblichen. Folgende Formen finden sich häufig bei lyrischen Texten.

Syntaktische Form	Beispiel
Chiasmus *(chiasmus)*: Überkreuzung oder Umdrehung von Wörtern oder Satzteilen	Beauty is truth, truth beauty.
Ellipse *(ellipis)*: Ein Teil des Satzes wird weggelassen, aber der Satz ist noch verständlich.	Jack ate several cookies but I didn't eat any.
Inversion *(inversion)*: Eine Umkehrung des üblichen Satzbaus	They sailed the ocean blue.
Parallelismus *(parallelism)*: Sätze oder Satzteile, in denen die Satzglieder dieselbe Abfolge haben.	I would not eat them here or there. I would not eat them anywhere. *(Dr. Seuss, Green Eggs and Ham)*

Metrik

GRUNDBEGRIFFE DER METRIK

- **Versfuß *(foot)* =** eine betonte Silbe und eine oder mehr unbetonte Silben, zwei oder drei Silben ergeben einen Versfuß
- **Versmaß/Metrum *(metre)* =** beschreibt die Verteilung/Anordnung der Versfüße in einer Zeile, also die Abfolge von betonten und unbetonten Silben
- **Strophe *(stanza)* =** eine Gruppe von Zeilen innerhalb eines Gedichts, meistens durch eine Leerzeile von der nächsten Strophe getrennt
- **Reimschema *(rhyming scheme)* =** die verschiedene Gruppierungen von Endreimen werden durch Buchstaben beschrieben (z. B. aa bb, abab, cdcd)
- **Vers =** eine Zeile eines Gedichts

Es gibt verschiedene Arten von **Versfüßen** in Gedichten, die an ihrem Muster von betonten und unbetonten Silben zu erkennen sind. Eine Wiederholung dieser Versfüße in einem Vers erfolgt oft nach einem erkennbaren Schema.

Versfuß	Beispiel
Amphibrach *(amphibrachic)* Rhythmus: da **dum** da	de**li**cious
Anapäst *(anapestic)* Rhythmus: da da **dum**	I like **salt** on my **chips**.
Daktylus *(dactyl/dactylic)* Rhythmus: **dum** da da	**Ma**laga
Jambus *(iamb/iambic)* Rhythmus: da **dum**	He **kicked** the **ball** and **scored** a goal.
Spondeus *(spondee/spondaic)* Rhythmus: **dum dum**	"**Cry, cry! Troy burns**, or else let Helen go." (Shakespeare, *Troilus and Cressida*)
Trochäus *(trochee/trochaic)* Rhythmus: **dum** da	**Twink**le, **twink**le, **litt**le star

Es wird auch danach unterschieden, wie oft sich die Versfüße in einem Vers (also einer Zeile) wiederholen.

Anzahl an Versfüßen	Versmaß
1	Monometer *(monometer)*
2	Dimeter *(dimeter)*

Anzahl an Versfüßen	Versmaß
3	Trimeter *(trimeter)*
4	Tetrameter *(tetrameter)*
5	Pentameter *(pentameter)*
6	Hexameter *(hexameter)*

In englisch-sprachigen Gedichten ist *iambic pentameter* ein sehr häufiger Betonungsmuster, also fünf Gruppen von jeweils zwei Silben, die erste unbetont und die zweite betont.

WEITERE BEGRIFFE DER METRIK

- Eine **Zäsur** *(caesura)* ist eine Unterbrechung – (Sprech-)Pause, sie wird oft mit einem Gedankenstrich, Doppelpunkt oder Strichpunkt angekündigt.
- Wenn ein Satz über das Ende einer Zeile in die nächste Zeile oder Strophe weitergeht, nennt man das **Enjambement**/Zeilensprung *(enjambement)*.

Abi Tipp

BEWUSSTE „STÖRUNG“

Wie in der Musik kann der Rhythmus eines Gedichts bewusst „gestört“ werden. So kann die Aufmerksamkeit des Lesers durch eine Änderung im Rhythmus auf bestimmte Wörter oder Phrasen gelenkt werden. Das sind dann Stellen, die oft von besonderer Wichtigkeit sind.

Die **Strophen** eines Gedichts erkennt man meistens visuell: Sie werden mit Leerzeilen voneinander getrennt.

Anzahl an Versen pro Strophe	Bezeichnung
3 Verse pro Strophe	Terzett *(tercet)*
4 Verse pro Strophe	Quartett *(quatrain)*
6 Verse pro Strophe	Sextett *(sestet)*
8 Verse pro Strophe	Oktett *(octave)*

Es ist wichtig, sich der verschiedenen möglichen **Reimschemen** bewusst zu sein, um diese bei der Gedichtanalyse identifizieren zu können.

Häufige Endreim-Muster	Reimschema
Paarreim *(rhyming couplet)* Zwei aufeinanderfolgende Verse reimen.	aa bb cc
Kreuzreim *(alternate rhyme)* Zwei alternierende Verse reimen.	abab cdcd efef
umarmender Reim *(embracing rhyme)* ein Paarreim umgeben von zwei reimenden Versen	abba cddc effe
Schweifreim *(tail rhyme)* ein Paarreim und ein umarmender Reim kombiniert	aab ccb ddb
Kettenreim *(chain rhyme)* Der mittlere Vers einer dreizeiligen Strophe reimt sich mit dem ersten und letzten Vers der nächsten Strophe.	aba bcb cdc

Reimarten

- **Stabreim** *(alliteration)*: eine ältere Form, betonte Wörter werden durch gleich Anlaute hervorgehoben
  → The **b**old **b**oy **b**attled **b**ravely.
- **Endreim** *(end rhyme)*: Gleichklang letzter Silben am Versende
  → She shed a tear and gave a **sigh**/As they said their last good**bye**.
- **männlicher/stumpfer Reim** *(masculine rhyme)*: In der englischen Verslehre der Gleichklang zweier einzelner Silben oder in betonter Schlussposition.
  → **fail/trail;** ap**peal**/un**real**
- **weiblicher/klingender Reim** *(feminine rhyme)*: Der Gleichklang von betonten Silben, gefolgt von mindestens einer unbetonten.
  → **fight**ing/**bit**ing; **green**ery/**scen**ery
- **Konsonanz** *(consonance)*: Konsonanten-Gleichklang in einem Vers
  → The **s**un **s**et over the **s**tormy **s**ea.
- **historischer Reim** *(historical rhyme)*: Zum Zeitpunkt des Schreibens reimten sich die Worte, durch zwischenzeitlich gewandelte Aussprache tun sie das heute nicht mehr.
  → "If this be error and upon me **proved**, I never writ, nor no man ever **loved**." (Shakespeare, Sonnet 116)

Häufig verwendete Stilmittel lyrischer Texte

Stilmittel	Beispiel
Alliteration *(alliteration)* = Eine Reihe von Wörtern, die mit dem gleichen Laut beginnen.	She sells seashells on the sea shore.
Euphemismus *(euphemism)* = eine mildere, beschönigende Art etwas auszudrücken, das peinlich, negativ bewertet oder tabuisiert ist	My grandfather **passed away** a few months ago.
Hendiadyoin *(hendiadys)* = Zwei semantisch ungleichwertige Worte werden mit „und" gekoppelt. Die Wirkung ist eine bekräftigende oder betonende.	Let's **go and visit** Mary this evening.
Hyperbel *(hyperbole)* = Übertreibung als rhetorisches Mittel	I've told you **a thousand times** to stop doing that!
Metapher *(metaphor)* = indirekter Vergleich. Ein Wort oder eine Wortgruppe wird dabei aus dem eigentlichen Bedeutungszusammenhang in einen neuen gehoben.	Sally is a **couch potato**.
Metonymie *(metonymy)* = Ein sprachlicher Ausdruck wird neu in einem nichtwörtlichen, übertragenen Sinn gebraucht, dabei muss eine inhaltliche Nachbarschaft zwischen dem wörtlichen und dem übertragenen Sinn bestehen.	They were speaking in their mother **tongue**.
Onomatopöie *(onomatapeoia)* = Worte ahmen Laute nach (Lautmalerei).	The meat **sizzled** on the hot barbecue.
Oxymoron *(oxymoron)* = eine Verbindung von zwei gegensätzlichen Begriffen Paradoxon *(paradox)* = eine Verbindung von Worten oder Phrasen, die auf den ersten Blick widersprüchlich sind	There was a **deafening silence** when the headteacher walked into the room. It was **the beginning of the end** for their relationship.

Stilmittel	Beispiel
Personifikation *(personification)* = Einem Gegenstand oder einer abstrakten Idee werden menschliche Charakterzüge verliehen.	The wind **sighed** in the trees.
Synekdoche *(synecdoche)* = Ein Teil repräsentiert ein Ganzes oder umgekehrt.	**England** played very well in their last match.

Wortwiederholungen

- Anapher *(anaphora)*: Wiederholungen am Anfang eines Satzes oder Verses
  → **It was** the best of times, **it was** the worst of times ...
- Epipher *(epiphora)*: Wiederholungen am Ende eines Satzes oder Verses
  → I love **football**, she loves **football**, everybody loves **football!**
- Epanalepse *(epanalepsis)*: Der Anfang eines Satzes oder Satzteils wird am Ende des Satzes wiederholt.
  → **The Queen** is dead; long live **the Queen!**
- Polyptoton *(polyptoton)*: Wiederholung von Wörter mit derselben Wurzel
  → It was the kind of day that made **life** worth **living**.

GEDICHTANALYSE — Checkliste

→ Wer ist das lyrische Ich?
→ Wie ist das Gedicht strukturiert?
→ Kommt ein spezieller Satzbau vor?
→ Reimt sich das Gedicht? Welches Reimschema wird verwendet?
→ Kommen andere Reimarten außer Endreim vor?
→ Welcher Versfuß ist zu erkennen?
→ Welche Stilmittel hat der Dichter verwendet und welche Wirkung haben sie?

Dramatik *(drama)*

GRUNDBEGRIFFE

- Dramen haben folgende Grundelemente:
  - **Thema/Stoff**. Beide Begriffe stehen auch in Konkurrenz zu Idee oder Motiv.
  - **Handlung/Geschehen** *(plot)*. Nötig sind handelnde Personen, Schauplatz und ein zeitlicher Ablauf mit einem Anfang und Ende.
  - In einem Theaterstück wird die Handlung im Wesentlichen durch **Dialoge** (Rede/Gegenrede) durch **Monologe** und mündliche **Berichte** vorangetrieben.
  - Handelnde Personen sind Schauspieler, die eine Rolle spielen, eine **Figur** *(character)* verkörpern. Es gibt ***round characters***, die vielschichtig dargestellt werden und lebensecht ausgestaltet sind (meistens die Hauptfiguren). In Kontrast dazu gibt es ***flat characters***, die eher eindimensional ausgeformt sind und deren Handeln leicht vorhersehbar ist.
  - Das **Bühnenbild** gibt der Handlung einen räumlichen Rahmen. Zusätzlich kann es das Geschehen zeitlich verorten. Etwa indem es Historisches abbildet.
  - Das Geschehen auf der Bühne kann **akustisch** unterstützt werden (Donner, Lärm, Musik).

Alle dieser Elemente sind bei einer Analyse von Belang.

- **Textgestalt** des Dramas: Es gibt den **Haupttext**, dieser gibt alles Gesprochene wieder. Der sogenannte **Nebentext** besteht unter anderem aus: Bühnenanweisung zur Gestaltung des Schauplatzes, Anweisungen zum Aussehen der Charaktere oder Hinweise zur Art des gewünschten Spiels (Mimik, Gestik). Alle Elemente des Nebentextes müssen bei der Analyse eines Dramas ebenfalls berücksichtigt werden.

Einteilung und Aufbau der Dramen

Schon in der Antike hat man Dramen in die beiden Gattungen Tragödie und Komödie aufgeteilt.

Gattung	Allgemeine Merkmale
Tragödie *(tragedy)*	Der Held muss einen schicksalhaften Konflikt durchmachen und stürzt dabei ab. Er kann dieses Schicksal nicht vermeiden und wird für seine Fehler bestraft. Ein Beispiel ist Shakespeares *Romeo and Juliet.*
Rachetragödie *(revenge tragedy)*	Der Held versucht, ein Unrecht wiedergutzumachen und begeht dabei selbst ein Unrecht. Die Tragödie besteht darin, dass er diese Situation nicht lösen kann und dabei sterben muss. Ein Beispiel ist Shakespeares *Othello*.
Komödie *(comedy)*	Die Handlung des Stückes soll die Zuschauer erheitern. Es kommen Charaktere aus den unteren Schichten vor, die in alltäglichen Situationen ihre menschlichen Schwächen zeigen. Ein Beispiel ist Shakespeares *Much Ado About Nothing*.
Restaurationskomödie *(restoration comedy)*	Nach der Hinrichtung von Charles I war England von 1649 bis 1660 eine Republik. Während dieser Zeit waren Theateraufführungen von der puritanischen Regierung verboten. 1660 wurde die Monarchie wieder eingeführt *(the Restoration)* und die Theater wieder geöffnet. Die Stücke, die zu dieser Zeit geschrieben wurden, scheuten sich nicht, sexuelle Themen und „Laster" wie Trinken und Glückspiele darzustellen. Böse Figuren blieben auch oft unbestraft; stattdessen wurden sie zu Helden des Stuckes. Ein Beispiel ist William *Wycherleys The Country Wife*.

Abi Tipp

GUT ZU WISSEN:

Bei Tragödien gibt es oft Nebenfiguren, die für ***comic relief*** sorgen. Diese Figuren sind oft Karikaturen, z. B. der Pförtner bei *Macbeth*. Die Figur erzählt Witze und macht sich lächerlich. Die Zuschauer können kurz „durchatmen", haben eine Pause beim Durchleiden des tragischen Geschehens.

Viele Dramen folgen einem bestimmten Aufbauschema.

Aufbau eines Dramas

- Exposition *(exposition)*
→ Einführung in die Thematik und Grundstimmung des Stückes. Die Zuschauer bekommen einen Einblick in die Figuren und die Ausgangssituation des Dramas.
- steigende Handlung *(rising action)*
→ Die Spannung steigt und die Handlung setzt sich fort.
- Höhepunkt *(climax)*
→ Der Konflikt des Stückes spitzt sich zu und erreicht seinen Höhepunkt. Meist ist dieser Höhepunkt auf eine einzige Szene konzentriert.
- fallende Handlung *(falling action)*
→ Die Spannung lässt nach und den Zuschauern wird signalisiert, dass der Konflikt bald gelöst sein wird.
- Ende *(ending)*
→ Die Lösung des Konflikts. Bei einer Tragödie ist dies im Regelfall der Tod des Helds. Bei einer Komödie kann es das gegenseitige Bekenntnis der Hauptfiguren sein, ineinander verliebt zu sein.

Die Sprache des Dramas

Natürlich spielt Sprache bei einem Theaterstück eine sehr wichtige Rolle. Analysieren Sie, wie diese verwendet wird.

Begriff	Beschreibung
Dialog *(dialogue)*	Zwei oder mehr Figuren reden miteinander. Die Handlung wird dadurch vorangetrieben.
Monolog *(monologue)*	Eine Figur spricht alleine ohne Interaktion mit anderen Figuren. Die Zuschauer bekommen Einblicke in die inneren Gedanken und den Geisteszustand der Figur. Weil Monologe zu wichtigen Zeitpunkten in der Handlung vorkommen, sollte man sie besonders beachten.
Selbstgespräch *(soliloquy)*	Bei einem *soliloquy* befindet sich die sprechende Figur alleine auf der Bühne. Hier enthüllt der Charakter den Zuschauer oft etwas über seine Gedanken oder Vorhaben.
Beiseitesprechen *(aside)*	In einem *aside* werden den Zuschauer Informationen gegeben, indem eine Figur etwas sagt, ohne dass die anderen Figuren dies hören. Dadurch bekommen die Zuschauer wichtige Informationen, die manchem Mitspieler auf der Bühne fehlen.

Begriff	Beschreibung
Mauerschau *(teichoscopy)*	Es kann nicht alles auf der Bühne gezeigt werden, was für den Fortgang der Ereignisse wichtig ist. Manche Ereignisse sind zu grausam (z. B. ein Mord) oder aus technischen Gründen nicht darstellbar (z. B. eine große Schlacht). Dieses Problem wird durch die sogenannte Mauerschau umgangen, indem eine Figur den Zuschauern berichtet, was diese nicht sehen können.
Botenbericht *(messenger's report)*	Boten werden auch dazu verwendet, Informationen zu übermitteln und über Dinge zu berichten, die abseits des auf der Bühne darstellbaren Raums geschehen. Zum Beispiel kann ein Bote über den Ausgang einer Schlacht oder über den Tod einer wichtigen Figur berichten.

Zu Shakespeares Zeit diente die Sprache zur Diffenzierung der Charaktere.

- **Metrisch geformte** oder **gereimte** Sprache signalisiert eine Figur aus einer **höheren Gesellschaftsschicht**.
- **Komische Figuren** aus den unteren Schichten verwenden eher **alltägliche Sprache**.

Eine Szene oder ein Akt wurde damals oft mit einem ***heroic couplet***, also zwei gereimten jambischen Pentametern, abgeschlossen. Dies signalisierte den Zuschauern, dass jetzt ein neuer Abschnitt kommt.

Gegen Ende der Renaissance bis hin zur Moderne wurde die Verwendung von ***blank verse*** (ein ungereimter fünfhebiger Jambus) immer beliebter.

- Diese Art Sprache ist noch **metrisch strukturiert**, bewegt sich aber vom **gereimten Vers** weg.

Die **ungereimte, nicht metrische Sprache**, die sich daraus entwickelte, wird ***free verse*** genannt.

Moderne Dramen verwenden normalerweise eine **alltägliche** Sprache.

- Bereits ab dem 19. Jahrhundert ist eine **realistische** Sprache ohne Reim oder besonderen Rhythmus Standard.
- Durch die **natürliche** Sprache wird immer noch zwischen Sozialschichten unterschieden. Wortwahl und Grammatik sind ausdifferenzierende Kennzeichen.
- Ab dem 20. Jahrhundert reflektiert die Sprache in Theaterstücke noch genauer, wie Menschen im wirklichen Leben sprechen. Zum Beispiel werden Sätze abgebrochen oder lange Pausen eingefügt.

BÜHNENANWEISUNGEN *(STAGE DIRECTIONS)*

Natürlich besteht ein Theaterstück aus mehr als nur Dialogen und Monologen. Durch die **Bühnenanweisungen** bekommen die Schauspieler und der Regisseur wichtige zusätzliche Informationen zu Mimik und Gestik, Kostüm, Musik und anderen akustischen Elementen sowie dem Bühnenbild.
Bühnenanweisungen werden *kursiv* geschrieben und in Klammern gesetzt, um sie vom Dialog zu unterscheiden.

Art der Bühnenanweisung	Bespiele
visuelle Anweisungen für die Schauspieler	**Handlungen** *(actions)*: *(Helen picks up the phone and listens for a moment.)* **Gestik** *(gestures)*: *(Tom beckons the waiter.)* **Mimik** *(facial expression)*: *(Sally frowns.)* **Kostüm** *(costume)*: *(She is wearing a long evening dress and high-heeled shoes.)*
akustische Anweisungen für die Schauspieler	**Stimme** *(voice)*: *Jim (whispering)*: Come here. **Sprachmelodie** *(intonation)*: *Tony (sarcastically)*: Oh, sure, that's a great idea.
visuelle Anweisungen für die Bühne	**Bühnenbild** *(stage design)*: *(The living room of Henry and Julia Thompson, which is furnished with an old, worn sofa and a couple of wooden chairs.)* **Kulisse** *(scenery)*: *(There is a large window at the back, through which we can see an overgrown garden.)* **Beleuchtung** *(lighting)*: *(The stage is in darkness. Gradually, a light comes on to reveal Ruth sitting in a rocking chair.)* **Requisiten** *(props)*: *(The table is set for a meal, with plates, cutlery, wine glasses and linen napkins.)*

Art der Bühnenanweisung	Bespiele
akustische Anweisungen für die Bühne	**Musik** *(music)*: *(The "Blue Danube" waltz is playing quietly in the background.)* **Geräusch** *(sounds)*: *(Larry exits. Gunfire is heard.)*

DRAMATISCHE IRONIE *(DRAMATIC IRONY)*

Man spricht von dramatischer Ironie, wenn die Zuschauer Informationen bekommen, die die Figuren auf der Bühne nicht erhalten.

- Die Zuschauer verstehen die Auswirkungen einer bestimmten Situation; die Figuren auf der Bühne sind aber über deren eigentliche Bedeutung nicht informiert.
- Dadurch entsteht Spannung: Die Zuschauer wollen wissen, wie die Figuren mit der besagten Situation zurechtkommen werden.
- Die Zuschauer bekommen dieses Wissen durch Beiseitesprechen oder durch Monologe auf der Bühne.
- In manchen Stücken, zum Beispiel bei *Romeo and Juliet*, werden die Zuschauer gleich am Anfang über den Ausgang der Geschichte informiert, in dem Fall durch den Chor.

ANALYSE VON DRAMEN — Checkliste

- → Welche Dramengattung liegt vor?
- → Was passiert am Höhepunkt des Stückes?
- → Welche Figuren sind *round characters* und welche sind eher *flat characters*?
- → Spricht eine Figur einen Monolog? Was für eine Wirkung hat dieser? Was lernen die Zuschauer daraus?
- → Sprechen die Figuren in Reimen oder in *blank verse*?
- → Wird dramatische Ironie verwendet?
- → Ist die verwendete Sprache realistisch oder stilisiert?
- → Welche Bühnenanweisungen sind wichtig zu erwähnen?
- → Wird eine bestimmte Beleuchtung vorgegeben und welche Wirkung hat sie?

Erzählende Literatur/Epik *(narration)*

GRUNDBEGRIFFE

- Epik ist neben Lyrik und Dramatik die dritte literarische Gattung.
- Es sind erzählende Texte in Vers- oder Prosaform.

→ Beispiele: Romane, Kurzgeschichten, Saga, Sprichwort, Legende

Romane *(novels)*

Merkmale:

- Der Text ist lang.
- Der Text ist oft in Kapitel aufgeteilt.
- Die Erzählung deckt oft lange Zeiträume ab.
- Es gibt viele Haupt- und Nebenfiguren; die Figuren sind vielseitig und komplex.
- Neben der Haupthandlung erlaubt der Umfang des Romans auch parallele Nebenhandlungen.
- Der Roman erzählt oft sehr detailreich. Er bietet unter anderem Raum für genaue Orts- oder Personenbeschreibungen. Auch kann vieles über soziale Hintergründe eingebracht werden.
- Es gibt sehr viele Romangattungen (etwa Science-Fiction und Schauerroman *(gothic novel)*, Liebesroman oder Krimi). Inzwischen gibt es sogar eine Gattung, die sich spezifisch an junge Erwachsene richtet: *young adult (YA) novels. The Hunger Games* von Suzanne Collins ist ein solcher Romn.

Beispiele:

→ Harper Lee, *To Kill a Mockingbird*

→ Aldous Huxley, *Brave New World*

→ F. Scott Fitzgerald, *The Great Gatsby*

Kurzromane *(novellas)*

Merkmale:

- Der Text ist kürzer als bei einem Roman, typischerweise umfasst der Text 60 bis 120 Buchseiten.
- Der Text wird meistens nicht in Kapiteln aufgeteilt.
- Es kommen wenige Figuren vor.
- Der Leser erfährt im Regelfall wenig zur Vorgeschichte.
- Es gibt weniger Konflikte und Nebenhandlungen.
- Meist steht ein einzelnes Ereignis im Fokus der Handlung.

Beispiele:

→ John Steinbeck, *Of Mice and Men*
→ Ernest Hemingway, *The Old Man and the Sea*

Kurzgeschichten *(short stories)*

Merkmale:

- Die Handlung istauf ein wichtiges Ereignis konzentriet.
- Die Handlung setzt sofort ein, es gibt keine detaillierte Beschreibung der Ausgangssituation.
- Es kommen wenige Figuren vor.
- Diese machen keine Entwicklung durch.
- Es gibt meist nur einen Schauplatz und die Handlung beschränkt sich auf einen kurzen Zeitraum.

Beispiele:

→ George Orwell, *Shooting an Elephant*
→ Doris Lessing, *The Second Hut*

Gattungen und Genres von Erzähltexte

Beschreibung	Beispiel
Science-Fiction *(science fiction)*: Beschreibung einer Zukunft, meist mit Schilderungen naturwissenschaftlicher oder technischer Fortschritte. Diese zukünftige Welt unterscheidet sich meist deutlich von den Gegebenheiten der Gegenwart. Science Fiction kann utopische oder dystopische Element enthalten.	Mary Shelley, *Frankenstein* H.G. Wells, *The Time Machine*

Beschreibung	Beispiel
Utopie *(utopia)* Utopische Literatur beschreibt eine ideale zukünftige Welt. Gesellschaftliche und politische Strukturen dieser Welt sind Hauptthema.	Ernest Callenbach, *Ectopia: The Notebooks and Reports of William Weston* Oliver Onions, *The New Moon: A Romance of Reconstruction*
Dystopie *(dystopia)* Die Menschen leben in einer (meist) unfreien Gesellschaft, in der sie sehr leiden müssen. Die Geschichte spielt meistens in einer totalitären oder postapokalyptischen Welt.	Margaret Attwood, *The Handmaid's Tale* George Orwell, *1984*
Mimesis *(mimesis)*: Realismus: Die Geschichte ahmt das wirkliche Leben nach.	Charles Dickens, *Hard Times* Nick Hornby, *About a Boy*
Poiesis *(poiesis/fantasy)*: Die Geschichte spielt in einer fantastischen Welt. Fantastische Wesen wie Elfe oder Drachen sind Elemente der Erzählung.	J.R.R. Tolkien, *The Hobbit* J.K. Rowling, *Harry Potter and the Philosopher's Stone*

Weitere wichtige Elemente der Analyse

STORY UND *DISCOURSE*

- Story bezieht sich darauf, **was** passiert.
- Discourse bezieht sich darauf, **wie** die Geschichte erzählt wird = etwa wer spricht, aus wessen Perspektive wird die Geschichte erzählt, in welchem Stil ist sie geschrieben, usw.

Es wird zwischen *story time* und *discourse time* unterschieden:
***Story time* (erzählte Zeit) =** die Abfolge der Ereignisse und die Zeit, die in der Erzählung vergeht.
***Discourse time* (Erzählzeit) =** die Zeit, die benötigt wird, um ein Ereignis zu erzählen.

Im Folgenden finden Sie andere Elemente, die Sie bei der Analyse von Erzähltexten beachten können.

Aspekte der Handlung *(plot)*

- *kernels* = entscheidende Aspekte einer Handlung, wie erstes Treffen der Hauptfiguren, Konflikte, ...
- *satellites* = Aspekte, die für die Handlung unwichtig sind, die als Abschweifung von der Haupthandlung dienen
- *sequence* = die (nicht unbedingt chronologische) Reihenfolge von Ereignissen in einer Geschichte
- *key events* = die wichtigsten Momente in einer Geschichte, die für den Weiterverlauf der Handlung entscheidend sind
- *theme* = das allgemeine Thema der Geschichte kann beispielsweise Liebe, Eifersucht oder Verlust sein
- *characters* = die Figuren, die in der Geschichte vorkommen

Erzählsituation *(narrative point of view)*

- *authorial narrative situation* (auktoriale Erzählsituation)

→ Der Erzähler ist allwissend und steht außerhalb der Handlung. Er kennt die Vorgeschichte und weiß, wie die Geschichte endet. Er kennt auch die Gedanken der Handelnden.

→ Beispiel: Jane Austen, *Emma*

- *first person narrator* (Ich-Erzählsituation)

→ Der Erzähler tritt als „I" in der Erzählung auf; er ist normalerweise an den beschriebenen Ereignissen beteiligt. Ein solcher Erzähler kann unzuverlässig sein, etwa, weil er nur seine Sicht auf das Ereignis darstellt oder dem Leser sogar Informationen verheimlicht.

→ Beispiel: J.D. Salinger, *The Catcher in the Rye*

- *figural narrative situation* (personale Erzählsituation)

→ Das Erzählen kann keiner bestimmten Figur zugeordnet werden. Verschiedene Figuren „erzählen". Durch diese variable Perspektive erfährt der Leser, wie verschiedene Figuren die Ereignisse der Geschichte erleben und ihre Sicht dazu. Dies verschafft den Leser ein Gesamtbild der Ereignisse.

→ Beispiel: Virginia Woolf, *Mrs Dalloway*

Der Autor/die Autorin hat verschiedene Möglichkeiten, die Figuren und deren inneres Leben darzustellen:

Darstellung der Figuren *(presentation of the characters)*

- *Showing*
  → Der Erzähler erklärt nicht, was die Figuren denken und fühlen. Stattdessen muss der Leser dies erschließen.
- *Telling*
  → Der Erzähler erklärt direkt, was die Figuren denken und fühlen. Der Leser muss nichts selbst interpretieren.

Der Unterschied zwischen *showing* und *telling*

→ *Showing: "I never want to see you again!" Jane marched out of the room, slamming the door behind her.*

→ *Telling: Jane was furious with Alan. "I never want to see you again!" she yelled.*

- *Interior monologue* (innerer Monolog)
  → Die innere Stimme einer Figur. Ihre Gedanken fließen unzensiert und der Leser erfährt viel über seinen Geisteszustand.
- *Psycho-narration* (Gedankenbericht)
  → Kommt bei der auktorialen Erzählsituation vor. Anders als beim inneren Monolog, berichtet der Erzähler hier von den Gedanken einer Figur.
- *Free indirect discourse* (erlebte Rede)
  → Eine Kombination der Stimme einer Figur und Kommentare des Erzählers. Die Worte, Gedanken und Gefühle der Figur werden über den Erzähler kommuniziert.

Beispiel:

Jenny hated the sound of the rain beating against the window. It meant she would have to wear her waterproofs to cycle to work and she thought they made her look ridiculous. It would just give Max another reason to laugh at her, to make her feel foolish in front of the others.

INTERPRETATION ERZÄHLENDER LITERATUR — Checkliste

→ Um welche Art Text handelt es sich?
→ Ist der Text einem Genre zuzuordnen?
→ Was ist die Erzählsituation des Textes?
→ Welche Art Erzähler liegt vor?
→ Gibt es einen oder mehrere Erzählstränge?
→ Wie ist der *plot* aufgebaut?
→ Wie werden die Charaktere dargestellt?

ANALYSE UND INTERPRETATION VON SACHTEXTEN

Sachtext-Typen

HÄUFIGE SACHTEXT-TYPEN

Wahrscheinlich wird der Sachtext, den Sie bearbeiten müssen, unter einer der folgenden Kategorien fallen:

- *political speeches,*
- *editorials,*
- *essays,*
- *reports.*

Political speech (politische Rede)

- Die Zuhörer sollen von einem bestimmten Standpunkt überzeugt werden.

Sie sollten bei der Analyse beachten:

- Was ist das Hauptthema?
- Welchen Standpunkt hat der Redner, bezogen auf das Hauptthema?
- Wer ist das Zielpublikum?
- Lässt der Redner eine bestimmte politische Grundorientierung erkennen? Ist er Vertreter eines bestimmten politischen Lagers, etwa als Politiker? Spricht der Redner diese Einordnung direkt aus? Oder muss sie indirekt aus dem Text erschlossen werden?
- Wie sind die Argumente strukturiert?
- Welche Redemittel werden verwendet, um die Zuhörer zu überzeugen?

Editorial (Leitartikel)

- Ein Artikel in einer Zeitung/einer Zeitschrift, der die Meinung eines Journalisten zu einem bestimmten Thema ausdrückt.

Sie sollten bei der Analyse beachten:

- Was ist das Hauptthema?
- Welche Argumente werden vorgebracht?
- Werden historische Ereignisse oder Personen erwähnt?
- Werden auffällige Stilmittel verwendet?
- Verwendet der Autor/die Autorin Zahlen, Daten oder andere Fakten, um sein Argument zu unterstreichen?
- Zitiert der Autor/die Autorin aus bestimmten Quellen?

Essay (Essay)

- Ein Essay ist ein geistreicher Text, in dem man sich mit einem Thema auf ganz persönliche Art auseinandersetzt. Essays behandeln oft kulturelle, gesellschaftliche/politische oder wissenschaftliche Themen.

Sie sollten bei der Analyse beachten:

- Um welche Form des Essays handelt es sich?

→ *comment* = Der Autor/die Autorin drückt seine/ihre Meinung zu einem Thema aus.

→ *argumentative essay* = Der Autor/die Autorin beschäftigt sich abwägend mit dem Für und Wider eines Themas und zieht abschließend ein Fazit.

→ *expository essay* = Der Autor/die Autorin erklärt oder verdeutlicht ein Thema für die Leser. Diese geschieht auf sachliche und möglichst objektive Weise. Der Autor beleuchtet dabei meist viele Aspekte.

Report (Bericht)

- Ein Bericht, normalerweise in einer Zeitung oder online veröffentlicht, der nicht dazu dient, eine Meinung auszudrücken. Stattdessen präsentiert er sachlich Informationen. Der Text ist neutral gehalten.

Sie sollten bei der Analyse beachten:

- Worum geht es in dem Text (Person/Sachverhalt/Ereignis)?
- Wann war das Ereignis, über das berichtet wird?
- Welches sind die Hintergründe?
- Welche Funktion und Aussage hat die Überschrift?
- Welchen Schluss zieht der Autor/die Autorin?

Sachtexte – der Inhalt

Der erste Schritt einer Sachtextanalyse ist im Regelfall eine kurze Zusammenfassung des Inhalts. In Ihren eigenen Worten geben Sie einen Überblick über die wichtigsten Aspekte des Textes.

Eine Zusammenfassung schreiben

- Lesen Sie den ganzen Text einmal durch.
- Unterstreichen oder markieren Sie dabei die wichtigsten Informationen.
- Nennen Sie im ersten Satz folgende Fakten zum Text:
  - → Textart/Textsorte
  - → Titel
  - → Autor/Autorin
  - → das Hauptthema
  - → falls Zeitungs-/Zeitschriften-/Online-Publikation, Erscheinungsdatum

Beispiel: *The political speech "I have a dream" was written and spoken by Martin Luther King, Jr., on August 28, 1963, and calls for equality for all people and an end to racism in the USA.*

- Die Zusammenfassung soll objektiv sein: keine Interpretation des Textes.
- Sie soll nur wichtige Fakten beinhalten; Einzelheiten wie Zahlen oder Zitate sind hier meist nicht relevant.
- Passen Sie auf, dass Ihr Text kurz bleibt und im Präsens geschrieben ist.

Thema	Beispiele
Die Intention des Autors	• *The author starts her essay with ... facts about/a quote from* • *He/She suggests that ...* • *He/She refers to ...* • *He/She highlights ...* • *He/She concludes that ...*
Vorstellung des Hauptthemas	• *The main subject/theme/topic of the article is ...* • *In this article, the author discusses ...* • *The author discusses the pros and cons of ...*

Analyse eines Sachtextes

Funktion des Textes

Funktion	Beispiele
argumentative (erörtend)	*This article is argumentative in style, as the author discusses the pros and cons of … /argues for and against …* *The purpose of this argumentative text seems to be to convince us that …*
descriptive (beschreibend)	*The text is descriptive in style, because it describes/shows us … / since it illustrates/depicts …*
expository (erklärend)	*The author has written an expository passage to inform the readers about/explain how/analyse the facts of …*
narrative (erzählend)	*The text is clearly narrative in style as it tells the story of …*

Abi Tipp

ÜBERSCHRIFT BEACHTEN!

Die Überschrift ist ein wichtiges Element des Gesamttextes. Sie deutet das Hauptthema des Textes an und signalisiert, in welchem Stil dieser geschrieben wurde (z. B. formell oder informell).

Beschreibung einer Überschrift

Formulierung der Überschrift:

- *The wording of the heading is shocking/dramatic/unclear/ambiguous/puzzling/confusing*
- *This headline is intended to interest/shock/baffle the readers …*

Der Titel eines Textes kann auch doppeldeutig sein, also ein Wortspiel *(pun)*. Dass eine Überschrift mehrdeutig ist, wird mitunter erst klar, nachdem man mehr vom Text gelesen hat.

Beispiel: *The article* Hungry for justice *describes Mahatma Gandhi's hunger strike in protest against the circumstances in India when it was a British colony. The text shows that the headline is meant both literally – Gandhi was hungry during his fight for justice – and metaphorically, because "to be hungry for something" means "to want something very much".*

DIE FUNKTION DES TEXTES

Was will der Text erreichen?

- belehren (*instruct*)
- beschreiben (*describe*)
- erörtern (*discuss/argue*)
- informieren (*inform*)
- überzeugen (*persuade/convince*)

Aufbau des Textes

Nach der Klärung der Funktion des Textes wenden Sie sich dessen Struktur zu.

- Wie viele **Absätze *(paragraphs)*, Abschnitte *(sections)*** oder **Teile *(parts)*** hat der Text?

The report is divided into four paragraphs.
This passage can be broken down into three parts.

- Worum geht es in den verschiedenen Teilen des Textes?
  The first paragraph describes ... In contrast, the second paragraph discusses ...
  In the first part of this extract, the author argues/compares ...
  The third section of the article deals with the author's opinion on ...
  In the final section of the text, the author concludes that ...

Sprachliche und inhaltliche Mittel

Es ist auch wichtig, die vom Autor verwendeten sprachlichen und inhaltlichen Mittel zu identifizieren und ihre Wirkung auf den Leser zu erklären. Diese Mittel können sachbezogen sein (z. B. die Verwendung von Statistiken, um ein Argument zu belegen) oder Stilmittel, die ihre Wirkung durch Sprache erzielen.

Devices used by the author	Effect on the reader
Use of numbers and other numerical data	*The reader feels that the text is well researched and that they can trust in what it says.*
Inclusion of quotes from experts	*The text seems more authentic.*
Use of rhetorical questions	*Makes the reader pay greater attention to what is being said.*
Use of "we", "us", "you"	*The reader feels they are being spoken to on a personal level; they are part of the discussion, not looking in from the outside.*
Use of repetition	*Draws attention to the message of the text and underlines it.*
Use of stylistic devices (e.g. metaphors etc)	*Paints a picture for the reader, stimulates their imagination.*
Use of irony or pun	*Often used to emphasize criticism; the reader knows that the author is being critical.*

Abi Tipp

ARGUMENTE BEGRÜNDEN

Denken Sie daran, dass Ihre persönliche Meinung **nicht** abgeprüft wird. Den Prüfer interessiert lediglich, ob Sie Argumente, die Sie vorbringen, sinnvoll, überzeugend und in fließendem Englisch begründen können.

Schlussfolgerung *(conclusion)*

Warum hat der Autor/die Autorin den Text geschrieben? Was will man den Lesenden vermitteln?

- In manchen Texte nennt der Autor/die Autorin klar, was er/sie sagen will.
- In anderen muss der Lesende dies indirekt erschließen.

Abschließend kommt Ihre Interpretation der Bedeutung des Textes. Das sollten Sie immer mit Bezug auf Gegebenheiten des Textes machen, etwa mit Zitaten aus dem Text.

Die Haltung des Autors/der Autorin beschreiben

The author

- *agrees* (stimmt zu)/*claims* (behauptet)/*implies* (deutet an)/*rejects* (lehnt ab)/*seems certain that* (scheint sicher zu sein)/*doubts whether* (zweifelt, ob) ...

The author's point of view is

- *optimistic/pessimistic*
- *snobbish* (hochnäsig/arrogant)
- *biased/unbiased* (befangen/unbefangen)

The author's attitude is

- *objective/subjective*
- *open-minded/prejudiced* (vorurteilsfrei/befangen)
- *compassionate/heartless* (mitfühlend/grausam oder kalt unbeteiligt)

ANALYSE UND INTERPRETATION VON SACHTEXTEN — Checkliste

→ Identifizieren Sie, um welche Art von Sachtext es sich handelt.
→ Was ist das Hauptthema des Textes?
→ Welchen Standpunkt hat der Autor/die Autorin?
→ Wurde der Text zu einem bestimmten Anlass geschrieben?
→ Soll der Text den Leser/die Leserin informieren/unterhalten/von etwas überzeugen?
→ Wo erschien der Text und wann wurde er geschrieben?
→ Was bedeutet die Überschrift?
→ Welche Funktion hat der Text?
→ Wie ist er strukturiert?
→ Welche Mittel wurden vom Autor/von der Autorin verwendet, damit der Text eine stärkere Wirkung hat?
→ Welche Schlüsse kann man aus dem Text ziehen?

11

ANALYSE UND INTERPRETATION VON VISUELLEN MATERIALIEN

Ein Bild beschreiben

Der erste Schritt ist eine genaue Beschreibung des Bildes. Dazu gehört beispielsweise:

- Um welche Art Bild handelt es sich (z. B. Foto)? Wenn Personen abgebildet sind, wie sehen sie aus? Was machen sie? Was passiert sonst auf dem Bild?

Es gilt hier nicht, das Bild zu interpretieren, sondern zu erklären, was darauf zu sehen ist!

Um welche Art Bild handelt es sich?

- a photo(graph)
- a painting
- an illustration
- a cartoon
- an electronic image
- a collage
- a still from a film

Wie leitet man eine Bildbeschreibung ein?

- Hier sind die wichtigsten Basisfakten zu erwähnen.

→ Beispiel: *This picture is a photograph of a group of people lying on the floor in a museum. It was published in the Guardian newspaper in April 2019 and shows people protesting against climate change.*

Useful phrases	Nützliche Redemittel
This photo reminds me of …	Das Foto erinnert mich an …
My first thought when I saw this painting was …	Mein erster Gedanke …

Useful phrases	Nützliche Redemittel
This image gives me the impression that ...	Bei diesem Bild bekomme ich den Eindruck, ...
The picture shows ...	Das Bild zeigt ...
In this still you can see ...	In diesem Standbild sieht man ...
This collage depicts ...	Diese Collage stellt .... dar.

Abi Tipp

DIE RICHTIGE ZEITFORM FÜR BILDBESCHREIBUNGEN

- Verwenden Sie das *simple present*, um zu beschreiben, was auf dem Bild zu sehen ist.

→ There are two men on the right-hand side of the photo.

- Verwenden Sie das *present* progressive, um zu beschreiben, was auf dem Bild passiert.

→ They are sitting at a table, drinking coffee.

Was sonst zu beachten ist:

- Beschreiben Sie die Menschen, die auf dem Bild zu sehen sind, anhand ihre **Gestik, Mimik**, ihrer **Körperhaltung** und ihres **Gesichtsausdrucks**.
- Beschreiben Sie zuerst den **Hauptaspekt** des Bildes, etwa die Person im Vordergrund oder ein Gebäude, bevor Sie den Hintergrund beschreiben.

Wo befinden sich die Gegenstände im Bild?

- *In the centre/In the foreground/In the background/At the front/back of the picture ...*
- *At the top/bottom/On the left-hand side/In the lower right-hand corner of the picture there is ...*

Welche Techniken wurden verwendet? Welche Eigenheiten sind zu erkennen?

- *The photograph is clear/out of focus/blurred.*
- *The colours are bright/dark/soft.*
- *The picture was created with water colours/oil paints/chalk.*
- *The artist used light brushstrokes/pencil to create an impression of ...*
- *The photographer took a close-up of/focussed on ...*

Welche Atmosphäre wurde erschaffen?

- *The use of ... creates a cheerful/lively/peaceful atmosphere.*
- *The atmosphere is gloomy/dark/frightening.*
- *These techniques give the picture a mysterious/chaotic/exotic feel.*
- *The artist has created a feeling of joy/sadness/despair.*

Wie wirk die Körpersprache der Menschen im Bild?

- *Her facial expression shows that she is surprised/angry/puzzled/happy/terrified.*
- *His body language implies that he is afraid/bored/nervous.*

Ein Bild interpretieren

Der nächste Schritt ist, das Bild zu analysieren: Welche Intention hatte der Künstler/der Fotograf/der Illustrator? Warum wurde das Bild in dieser Form erschaffen? Bedenken Sie dabei:

- Wie werden die **Menschen** im Bild dargestellt? Was sagt ihre **Körpersprache** über ihre **Gefühle** und ihre **Beziehung zu einander**?
- Steht das Bild im Zusammenhang mit einem **sozialen Problem** oder **historischen Ereignis**?
- Soll eine **Botschaft** vermittelt werden?
- Was für einen **Eindruck** macht das Bild auf die Personen, die es betrachten?

Redemittel zur Bildanalyse

- *This photo is about protests regarding climate change.*
- *The painting represents the problems of the refugee crisis.*
- *This illustration goes with the newspaper article about ...*
- *The image deals with gun crime in the USA.*

Redemittel zur Bildinterpretation

- *This still from the film ... gives you the impression that ...*
- *The photo implies/suggests that ...*
- *This cartoon criticizes ...*
- *Judging by the woman's body language ...*
- *From the look of the room, we can conclude that ...*

Redemittel zur Intention des Künstlers/der Künstlerin

- *The photographer wants to highlight the problem of ...*
- *The painter intended to illustrate certain aspects of ...*
- *The artists wants to express her anger about ...*
- *This cartoon is aimed at people who ...*

Abschließend sollten Sie Ihre Meinung zu dem Bild äußern. Welchen Eindruck macht das Bild auf Sie? Ihre Meinung kann positiv oder negativ sein; Sie müssen nur genau begründen, warum das Bild diese Wirkung auf Sie hat.

Die persönliche Meinung darlegen

Einige Formulierungen, die dabei nützlich sind:
- *In my opinion/To my mind/From my point of view ...*
- *The impression I get from this picture/cartoon/image is ...*
- *I like/am moved by/am touched by this picture because ...*
- *This image appeals/does not appeal to me because ...*
- *In conclusion/To sum up, I feel ...*

Sie können diese Formulierungen der Aufgabe einfach anpassen.

Eine Karikatur analysieren

EIGENSCHAFTEN VON KARIKATUREN

Karikaturen *(cartoons)* sind Bilder, die einen Sachverhalt überzeichnen, eben karikieren. Meist werden Karikaturen von einem Text begleitet. Dies kann in Form
- einer Sprechblase *(speech bubble)*,
- einer Bildunterschrift *(caption)* oder
- einer Beschilderung *(label)* geschehen.

Cartoons sind satirisch. Sie verspotten etwa Politiker und andere bekannte Persönlichkeiten.

Karikaturen verwenden viele Stilmittel, um ihre Botschaft zu vermitteln:
- Übertreibung (***exaggeration***)
- Ironie ***(irony)***

- Wortspiel ***(pun)***
- Vergleich ***(simile)***
- Symbol ***(symbol)***
- Metapher ***(metaphor)***

Arten von Karikaturen

- ***single-panel cartoons*** **=** besteht aus einem Bild mit Unterschrift
- ***comic strips*** **=** mehrere Bilder, die eine kurze Geschichte erzählen oder einen Witz machen
- ***editorial cartoons*** **=** begleiten einen Leitartikel in einer Zeitung oder einer Zeitschrift; das Thema ist oft ernster Natur. So werden beispielsweise politische Themen satirisch betrachtet.

Sie können viele der **Redemittel** für Bildbeschreibungen verwenden, um eine Karikatur zu beschreiben. Bedenken Sie, dass Sie hier zudem den dazugehörigen Text beachten müssen:

- *"The caption below the cartoon says ..."*
- *"In the first speech bubble, the man says ..."*
- Sie können den Text auch in indirekter Rede wiedergeben:
- *"There is a woman standing on the roof of her house in what looks like the middle of a river. She is saying that she does believe in climate change after all."*

Hilfreiche Fragen bei der Analyse einer Karikatur

- Where and when is the cartoon set?
- What do the characters' body and language and facial expressions tell us about their feelings and their relationships to one another?
- What is happening in the cartoon?
- Is the language used formal or informal?
- What symbols/metaphors/puns has the cartoonist used, if any?

Hilfreiche Redemittel

- The cartoon refers to/is about ...
- This cartoon satirises ...
- The main figure in the picture looks like/is a caricature of ...
- We can see from the person's body language/facial expression ...
- ... is a symbol of/represents ...
- The language in the speech bubble is very formal/informal ...

Im letzten Teil der Analyse zeigen Sie, dass Sie die Botschaft der Karikatur erkannt haben. Natürlich müssen Sie in die Analyse zudem Ihre eigene Meinung einbringen.

Was ist die Botschaft der Karikatur?

- The cartoonist is making fun of/satirising/making a sarcastic comment about ...
- She/He is criticising ...
- The artist is making the point that/wants to draw attention to ...
- He wants the reader to realise that ...

Filme analysieren

Aufbau einer Filmanalyse

Wichtige Elemente einer Filmanalayse sind:

- kurzer Überblick der Angaben zum Film (Titel, Regisseur/Regisseutrin, etc.),
- kurze Zusammenfassung der Handlung,
- Analyse eines (zumeist vorgegebenen) Filmausschnitts (was passiert, wo spielt die Szene, Atmosphäre, Verhalten der Charaktere, usw.),
- relevante Aspekte der Kinematographie.

Informationen zum Film	Beispiele
Titel, Erscheinungsjahr, Herkunftsland, Regisseur/Regisseurin, Hauptdarsteller/Hauptdarstellerin, Thematik	Crash is a 2004 film produced in the USA and directed by Paul Haggis. It stars an ensemble cast, including Sandra Bullock, Don Cheadle and Matt Dillon. It deals with social and racial tensions in Los Angeles.
Worum geht es in dem Film?	The film tells several parallel stories which intersect at different points ...
Wo spielt der Film und zu welcher Zeit?	The film is set in Los Angeles at the beginning of the 21st century.
Wer sind die Protagonisten?	The film has several main characters, ranging from a wealthy white couple to police officers and criminals.

Formulierungen zur Analyse eines Filmauschnitts

- The clip is tragic/surprising/shocking because ...
- The clip is set in ... before/during/after ...
- The atmosphere in this scene is frightening/uplifting/romantic/upsetting ...
- The characters in this clip are angry/rude/loving/in conflict with each other ...
- The woman in the clip is well-dressed/elegant/wearing old-fashioned clothes ...
- The characters speak to each other in slang/in formal language ...
- The protagonist's monologue reveals ...
- The woman speaks very quietly/nervously/aggressively ...
- The dialogue in this clip gives us important information about ...

Technische Aspekte des Films	Beispiele
Kameraführung *(camera operation)*	high/low angle; eye-level shot; close-up; long shot; tracking shot; shot with a hand-held camera
Schnitt *(cut)*	freeze frames; slow motion; fast cuts;
Beleuchtung *(lighting)*	black and white; low lighting; strong light; semi-darkness; warm/cold colours
Ton *(sound)*	music/musical score; background noise

ANALYSE UND INTERPRETATION VON VISUELLEN MATERIALIEN — Checkliste

→ zuerst das Bild im Detail beschreiben, dann seine Bedeutung analysieren und interpretieren
→ bei der Beschreibung auf das richtige Tempus achten (*simple present und present progressive*)
→ geeignete Redemittel verwenden, um einen flüssig zu lesenden Text zu schreiben
→ bedenken, dass die Bildunterschrift oder anderer Texte bei der Analyse berücksichtigt werden müssen
→ Die Filmanalyse hat ein ganz eigenes Vokabular, das Sie sich aneignen sollten.

KRITERIEN DER ZIELTEXTFORMATE

Brief *(letter)*

BRIEFE SCHREIBEN – WORAUF SOLL MAN ACHTEN?

- das Sprachregister – formell, neutral, informell
- eine klare Gliederung
- korrektes Layout für Adresse, Datumsangabe, Empfänger
- korrekte Anrede und Schlussformel, je nach Sprachregister

Formal letter (förmlicher Brief)

Sprachregister und Stil:

- *formal English*

Aufbau:

- **Einleitung:** Sie geben an, warum Sie diesen Brief schreiben (Sie beziehen sich auf das Thema in der Aufgabenstellung).
- **Hauptteil:** Sie äußern Ihr Anliegen, Sie argumentieren für oder gegen ein Thema, Sie informieren. Sie verwenden dabei *sentence connectives*, um einen flüssigen Text zu erstellen.
- **Schluss:** Sie fassen kurz zusammen; gegebenenfalls formulieren Sie, was Sie als nächsten Schritt vom Empfänger erwarten.

Letter to the editor (Leserbrief)

Sprachregister und Stil:

- (meist) *formal English*; das Sprachregister passt sich aber an die Art Publikation an, in der der Brief erscheinen soll.

Aufbau:

- **Einleitung:** Sie führen das Thema des Ausgangstextes an und geben Ihre Position dazu an.
- **Hauptteil:** Sie legen Ihre Argumente klar und verständlich dar. Sie verwenden dabei *sentence connectives* und *topic sentences*.
- **Schluss:** Sie fassen Ihre Argumente zusammen.

Personal letter (persönlicher Brief)

Sprachregister und Stil:
- *informal English*

Aufbau:
- **Einleitung:** Sie geben an, warum Sie den Brief schreiben und beziehen sich dabei auf den Inhalt des Ausgangstextes.
- **Hauptteil:** Je nach Aufgabenstellung erzählen Sie eine Geschichte, erklären Ihrem Freund etwas, machen Vorschläge (z. B. für eine gemeinsame Aktivität), geben Ratschläge, usw. Die passenden *sentence connectives* nicht vergessen!
- **Schluss:** Beenden Sie den Brief mit einer Frage, einem Vorschlag, einem Plan für ein Vorhaben, Grüße an ...

E-Mail

E-MAILS SCHREIBEN – WORAUF SOLL MAN ACHTEN?

- **Sprachregister =** Geht die E-Mail an einem Freund, einen Politiker, einen zukünftigen Arbeitgeber?
- **Betreffzeile =** Gibt an, worum es in der E-Mail geht.
- **Anrede und Schlussformel =** wie bei Briefen
- **Gliederung =** wie bei Briefen

E-mail (E-Mail)

Sprachregister und Stil:
- Je nach Adressat: alles von *formal* bis *informal style*

Aufbau:
- **Einleitung:** Sie nehmen Bezug auf das Thema der Aufgabe und geben an, weshalb Sie schreiben.
- **Hauptteil:** Sie legen – klar und verständlich strukturiert – die geforderten Informationen dar. Sie verwenden passende *sentence connectives, topic sentences* und *closing remarks*.
- **Schluss:** Sie fassen kurz zusammen. Je nach Aufgabenstellung können Sie hier schreiben, was Sie als nächsten Schritt vom Empfänger erwarten. Grußformel nicht vergessen.

Rede *(speech)*

DAS ZIEL EINER REDE

- die Zuhörer informieren
- die Zuhörer von etwas überzeugen
- ein Thema debattieren

Talk (Vortrag)

Sprachregister und Stil:

- *formal English*; es werden auch rhetorische Mittel eingesetzt

Aufbau:

- **Einleitung:** Der Redner/die Rednerin begrüßt die Zuhörer und stellt sich vor. Das Thema und das Ziel des Vortrags wird präsentiert.
- **Hauptteil:** Die relevante Informationen werden klar und verständlich dargestellt. Neben *sentence connectives* sollte der Redner/die Rednerin auch rhetorische Mittel verwenden, um die Zuhörer aufmerksam zu halten und zu überzeugen.
- **Schluss:** Der Redner/die Rednerin fasst die eigenen Ansichten zusammen. Man kann die Zuhörenden zum Handeln aufrufen. Am Ende bedankt man sich für die Aufmerksamkeit.

Public speech (öffentliche Rede)

Sprachregister und Stil:

- *formal English;* rhetorische Mittel; informelle Elemente

Aufbau:

- **Einleitung:** Der Redner/die Rednerin begrüßt die Zuhörer und stellt das Thema vor. Man nennt den Anlass/Grund für die Rede und auch das eigene Ziel.
- **Hauptteil:** Argumente werden präsentiert. Mit rhetorischen Mitteln versucht man, die Zuhörenden aufmerksam zu halten und zu überzeugen.
- **Schluss:** Zusammenfassung und Appell an die Zuhörer und Zuhörerinnen.

***Debate/Statement* (Debatte/Stellungnahme)**

Sprachregister und Stil:

- *formal English*; es werden auch rhetorische Mittel eingesetzt

Aufbau:

- **Einleitung:** Der Redner/die Rednerin begrüßt die Zuhörenden und präsentiert das Thema.
- **Hauptteil:** Man präsentiert die Argumente aus der eigenen Perspektive. Man nennt relevante Fakten und bringt Beispiele, die den eigenen Gesichtspunkt unterstützen.
- **Schluss:** Am Ende fasst man zusammen und appelliert an die Zuhörenden, den eingenommenen Standpunkt zu unterstützen.

Abi Tipp

ENGLISCH LESEN, HÖREN UND SEHEN!

Je öfter Sie Englisch lesen, je öfter Sie etwa Filme in Originalsprache sehen, desto vertrauter werden Sie mit verschiedenen Sprech- und Schreibstilen. Sie lernen dabei zudem, wie „natürliches" Englisch klingen soll. Versuchen Sie etwa, jeden Tag einen kurzen Text zu lesen – suchen Sie einfach online nach einem Artikel, der Sie interessiert. „Sprachkonsum" macht den Meister!

Berichte und Artikel *(reports and newspaper articles)*

ZEITUNGSARTIKEL – WORAUF SOLL MAN ACHTEN?

- Wo soll der Artikel erscheinen: *quality paper, tabloid, school magazine, online magazine, website, blog* ... ?
- Welches Sprachregister passt dazu?
- Schreiben Sie aus der Perspektive der eigenen Person oder übernehmen Sie eine Rolle?
- An wen ist der Text gerichtet?
- Was soll den Lesern und Leserinnen mitgeteilt werden?

Report (Bericht)

Sprachregister und Stil:

- *Formal English*; manchmal gibt es auch informelle Elemente, die bestimmte Lesende ansprechen sollen; der Still ist eher sachlich und objektiv.

Aufbau:

- **Einleitung:** Sie beginnen selbstverständlich mit einer passenden Überschrift; der erste Absatz führt ins Hauptthema.
- **Hauptteil:** Sie bearbeiten die Aufgabenstellung sachlich, mit klaren, verständlichen Argumenten. Sie gliedern den Bericht in logisch begründbare Absätze – ein Unterthema pro Absatz.
- **Schluss:** Ihre zusammenfassende Schlussaussage rundet Ihre Argumente ab.

Comment (Kommentar)

Sprachregister und Stil:

- *formal English*; teilweise mit informellen Elemente und gekonnt eingesetzten rhetorischen Mitteln

Aufbau:

- **Einleitung:** Sie führen ins Thema ein, basierend auf Hintergrundinformationen und Fragen, die zum Nachdenken anregen sollen.
- **Hauptteil:** Sie vertreten einen Standpunkt gemäß der Aufgabenstellung. Sie nutzen Fakten, Argumente und Beispiele, um Ihren Standpunkt glaubwürdiger zu machen.
- **Schluss:** Sie fassen Ihre Argumente zusammen. Man wird am Ende des Kommentars Ihren Standpunkt deutlich erkennen.

Interview (Interview)

Sprachregister und Stil:

- *informal English*; rhetorische Mittel
- Das Interview wird in Form eines Dialogs geschrieben.

Aufbau:

- **Einleitung:** Sie führen den Grund für das Gespräch ein. Sie begrüßen Ihren Gesprächspartner/ihre Gesprächspartnerin.
- **Hauptteil:** Sie schreiben einen klaren, verständlichen Dialog mit Fragen, Antworten, Fakten und Argumenten: Das Thema wird „ausdiskutiert“.
- **Schluss:** Sie fassen die Hauptpunkte zusammen und bedanken sich bei Ihrem Gesprächspartner/ihrer Gesprächspartnerin.

Literarische Texte *(literary texts)*

KREATIVE TEXTE ERSTELLEN

Typische Aufgabenstellungen sind:
- ein Ende oder eine Fortsetzung eines Textauszuges,
- ein alternatives Ende für einen Text,
- Neues aus der Sicht einer bestimmten Figur,
- Begebenheiten, die der Leser/die Leserin nicht vollständig kennt,

kreativ weiterentwickeln.

Narrative text (Erzählung)

Sprachregister und Tempus:
- hängt vom Ausgangstext ab
- Tempus des Ausgangstextes verwenden

Aufbau:
- **Einleitung:** Sie knüpfen an die Ausgangssituation, an den Schauplatz und die Zeit des Ausgangstextes an.
- **Hauptteil:** Sie erstellen einen kreativen Text, der auf schlüssige Weise die Aufgabenstellung erfüllt.
- **Schluss:** Sie runden den Text ab; eventuell kommen Sie noch einmal zu Elementen des Ausgangstexts zurück.

Drama (Schauspiel, Film)

Sprachregister und Tempus:
- hängt vom Ausgangstext ab
- meist im Präsens geschrieben

Aufbau:
- **Einleitung:** Sie knüpfen an die Ausgangssituation, an den Schauplatz und die Zeit des Ausgangstextes an.
- **Hauptteil:** Sie erstellen einen kreativen Text, der auf schlüssige Weise die Aufgabenstellung erfüllt.
- **Schluss:** Sie runden den Text ab; eventuell kommen Sie noch einmal zu Elementen des Ausgangstexts zurück.

Eine *composition* schreiben

VERSCHIEDENE ARTEN VON *COMPOSITIONS*

- ***comment* =** detaillierte Analyse eines Themas, inklusive eigenem Standpunkt; Argumente, unterstützt von Beispielen; mit eigener Meinung zum Thema abschließen
- ***essay* =** vertiefte Untersuchung eines Themas, Argumente für und gegen ein Thema darstellen
- ***interpretation* =** die Bedeutung eines literarischen Textes oder Sachtextes oder Bildes untersuchen; die Bedeutung von Symbolen und die bildhafte Sprache analysien; übergeordnete Bezüge präsentieren; die eigene Meinung darlegen

Eine gute Einleitung verfassen:

- Das Thema wird vorgestellt.
- Das Interesse der Lesenden wird geweckt: zu diesem Zweck, kann die Einleitung ein Zitat, eine provokative Aussage, eine rhetorische Frage, die Wiedergabe öffentlicher Meinung, Ihre eigene Meinung oder eine persönliche Erfahrung enthalten.

Nützliche Formulierungen	Beispiele
Einleitung	• *According to the latest statistics* • *It is a well-known fact that ...* • *It is often said that ...* • *Have you ever ...* • *Imagine this: there are*
Einführung des Themas	• *Many people believe that ...* • *Most people would agree that ...* • *It has often been claimed that ...*
Erklärung der Ausgangslage	• *The statement above claims ...* • *From this point of view ...* • *In general, this statement suggests ...*

Den Hauptteil gut planen:

Sie sollten immer etwas Zeit in die Planung Ihrer *composition* investieren. Sie haben verschiedene Techniken für das Sammeln von Ideen und deren Organisation gelernt, die Sie hier anwenden können. Um eine gute

Note zu bekommen, muss vor allem der Hauptteil des Aufsatzes klar strukturiert und logisch argumentierend sein.

- Notieren Sie Ideen, Argumente und Beispiele.
- Entscheiden Sie, welche Elemente dieser Sammlung Sie verwenden wollen und organisieren Sie diese in einer sinnvollen Reihenfolge.
- Formulieren Sie einen neuen Absatz für jedes neue Argument.
- Verwenden Sie Bindewörter, damit der Text flüssig und natürlich klingt.

Nützliche Formulierungen	Beispiele
Gründe nennen	• *This is due to ...* • *There are a few questions to consider when discussing ...* • *The reason is that ...* • *Some of the issues here are ...*
Argumente weiterführen	*above all, also, besides, in addition, furthermore, still, too*
Argumente auflisten	• *First of all, to start with, next, then, finally* • *Firstly ... secondly ... thirdly...* • *Last of all, last but not least ...*
Ähnlichkeiten hervorheben	*equally, likewise, similarly, in the same way*
Einschränkungen ausdrücken	*after all, although, even if, in any case, in spite of*
Bezugnahme ausdrücken	*concerning, looking at, referring to, regarding, related to*
zeitliche Bezüge nennen	*after, as soon as, at the same time, before, finally, from now on, in the future, in the past, meanwhile, now, nowadays, previously, recently, since, then, time and again*
Gegenteile oder Kontraste ausdrücken	*although, but, despite, however, in contrast to, in spite of, on the contrary, on the other hand, yet*
Beispiele geben	• *for example, for instance, in other words, such as* • *This is illustrated by ...* • *As most people know/It is common knowledge that ...*

Mit einem guten Schluss abrunden:

- Sie fassen Ihre Argumente kurz zusammen.
- Sie nennen Ihre eigene Meinung, inklusive die Gründe für Ihren Standpunkt.
- Sie sollten im Schlussteil keine neue Argumente einbringen!

Nützliche Formulierungen	Beispiele
Schlussteil	▪ *From my point of view/In my view …* ▪ *In my opinion …* ▪ *As a result …* ▪ *On the whole …* ▪ *finally, in conclusion, last of all, to sum up …*
Stellung nehmen	▪ *I firmly believe that …* ▪ *It seems to me that …* ▪ *I would like to point out that …* ▪ *If you ask me …* ▪ *I (dis)agree that …*
Schlussfolgerung	▪ *As a consequence/result …* ▪ *The logical result of this is …* ▪ *This is why …* ▪ *accordingly, consequently, therefore*

KRITERIEN DER ZIELTEXTFORMATE Checkliste

→ Machen Sie sich mit den verschiedenen Zieltextarten vertraut. Wie muss ein Brief/Kommentar/Bericht etc. formuliert werden?
→ Achten Sie auf eine klare Struktur des Textes: Einleitung, Hauptteil, Schluss.
→ Achten Sie auf das Sprachregister (formell, neutral, informell).
→ Passen die verwendeten rhetorischen Mittel zur Textart?
→ Ist der Text durch die Verwendung von *sentence connectives* flüssig zu lesen?
→ Planen Sie den Aufsatz genau, bevor Sie mit dem Schreiben beginnen.
→ Teilen Sie den Text in Absätze auf – beginnen Sie einen neuen Absatz für jedes neue Argument.
→ Verwenden Sie Formulierungen, die Sie im Unterricht gelernt haben.
→ Lesen Sie den fertigen Text sorgfältig durch, bevor Sie ihn abgeben.

13

LITERATURGESCHICHTE IM ÜBERBLICK

Renaissance & 16. Jahrhundert

BEDEUTENDE EINFLÜSSE AUF DIE LITERATUR

- Wiederentdeckung der Kunstformen der **Antike**
- Gutenbergs Erfindung des **Buchdrucks** (1448)
- die Verbreitung des Buchdrucks in England durch William Caxton
- die **Reformation** und Martin Luthers Übersetzung der Bibel

Wichtige Literaturformen der Epoche

das Sonett *(sonnet)*

- hat vierzehn Zeilen,
- die Thematik ist die Liebe.

Drama *(plays)*

- Königin Elizabeth I liebte das Theater. → Das englische Drama erlebte während ihrer Herrschaft eine Glanzzeit.
- wichtigster Autor: **William Shakespeare**

→ Vielfalt von Dramen: Historien, Romanzen, Komödien, Tragödien
→ Erfindung von Wörtern (Neologismen) und Redewendungen
→ spannende Geschichten und fesselnde Figuren
→ berühmte Werke: *Macbeth, Romeo and Juliet, A Midsummer Night's Dream, Hamlet, The Tempest*

Abi Tipp

SHAKESPEARE BESSER VERSTEHEN

Shakespeares Stücke sind nicht immer einfach zu verstehen: Es empfiehlt sich daher, eine der vielen Verfilmungen anzuschauen. Dadurch versteht man die Geschichte als Ganzes; viele Nuancen werden durch die Schauspieler auch deutlicher.

Das 17. Jahrhundert

DAS (VORÜBERGEHENDE) ENDE DES THEATERS

- 1649: King Charles I wird hingerichtet und das Land wird von einer **Militärherrschaft** unter Oliver Cromwell regiert.
- Die **puritanische Regierung verbietet Theateraufführungen** als frivolen Zeitvertreib und schließt alle Theater.
- Erst nach der ***Restauration***, als die Monarchie mit Charles II wiedereingeführt wird (1660), wird Theater wieder öffentlich gespielt

Wichtige Literaturformen der Epoche

Restaurationskomödie *(Restoration comedy)*
- unbeschwertes, nicht anspruchsvolles Drama = Reaktion auf die Zeit unter den Puritaner
- Figuren sind oft Typen, z. B. Schurken oder Einfaltspinsel, statt runde Figuren
- Schauspielerinnen und freizügige Thematik. Das wurde von manchen als unmoralisch betrachtet.

→ Beispiel: William Wycherly, *The Country Wife*

metaphysische Lyrik *(metaphysical poetry)*
- komplexe Sprache mit vielen Metaphern
- elitär: schwierig zu verstehen

→ Beispiel: Gedichte von John Donne

Höfische Dichtung *(cavalier poetry)*
- Verwendung von klassischen Formen
- weltliche Lebensansichten

→ Beispiel: John Milton, *Paradise Lost*

Romanzen *(romances)*
- Höfische Liebe; Ritter bekämpfen Fabelwesen, um das reine Herz einer Dame zu gewinnen.

→ Beispiel: Aphra Benn, *Oroonoko* = Beispiel eines frühen Romans einer Autorin

Prosa-Allegorie *(allegorical tale)*

→ Beispiel: John Bunyon, *The Pilgrim's Progress* = eine christliche Allegorie

Das 18. Jahrhundert

WICHTIGE ENTWICKLUNGEN

- Der englische **Roman** wird zur bedeutenden Literaturform.
- Ende des Jahrhunderts: Die **Romantik** signalisiert den Anfang einer ganz neuen Art von Kunst.
- Die vor Kurzem unabhängig gewordenen **USA** entwickelten ihre eigene Literatur.

Der Roman des 18. Jahrhunderts

- Ein immer größerer Teil der Bevölkerung kann lesen: Das Interesse an längeren Prosatexten steigt.
- *Robinson Crusoe* von Daniel Defoe (1719) wird als der erste englischen Roman betrachtet.

→ Die Geschichte handelt von einem normalen Mensch (= kein Adeliger) in einer ungewöhnlichen, aber nachvollziehbaren Situation. → Es gibt keine mythischen Elemente.

- Der Sprachstil ist alltäglich: Die Figuren sprechen wie im wirklichen Leben.

Die Romantik *(Romanticism)*

- Dichter wie William Wordsworth und Samuel Coleridge entwickeln eine neue Art von Lyrik.
- Ihre Gedichte werden in alltäglicher Sprache geschrieben.
- Ein häufiges Thema romantischer Lyrik ist die Natur.

Literatur in den USA

- In dem nun unabhängigen Land wollte man eine eigene Literatur entwickeln.
- Die Werke dieser Zeit reflektierten das Bewusstsein des neuen Landes: Sie drücken den Wunsch nach Unabhängigkeit aus, und sie beschreiben das Leben in der neuen Welt.

→ Beispiele: Thomas Paine, *Common Sense*; Benjamin Franklin, *Autobiography*; J. Hector St Jean de Crevecoeur, *Letters from an American Farmer*

Das 19. Jahrhundert

VIELFALT DER LITERATURARTEN

- **Schauerroman =** Phänomene, die schlecht erklärlich sind, werden thematisiert.
- **Die Rolle der Frau =** Romane, die von Frauen handeln und von Frauen geschrieben werden
- **Realismus =** Reaktion auf den Idealismus der Romantik
- **Ästhetizismus =** Suche nach dem Sinn der Kunst in der Schönheit
- Erste Hochphase der US-amerikanischen Literatur

Schauerroman *(gothic novel)*

- Die Wissenschaft begann, die Welt zu erklären.
- Der Schauerroman dagegen beschäftigt sich mit Dingen, die man nicht erklären konnte oder die tabu waren: Geister, als unnatürlich betrachteten Begierden, Sexualität.

→ Beispiel: Mary Shelley, *Frankenstein*

Der weibliche Roman

- Die Situation der Frau im 19. Jahrhundert wird vermehrt thematisiert und kritisch unter die Lupe genommen: Die Abhängigkeit von Männern, die Doppelmoral der viktorianischen Gesellschaft sind wichtige Themen.
- Immer mehr Frauen schreiben Romanen, die gerne von Frauen gelesen werden.

→ Beispiele: Jane Austen, *Pride and Prejudice*; Emily Brontë, *Wuthering Heights*

Realismus *(Realism)*

- Als Gegenreaktion zur Romantik befassen sich immer mehr Romane mit der harten Realität des Lebens für die Arbeiterklasse, die meistens nur die Nachteile der *Industrial Revolution* zu tragen hatte.
- Die Romane zeigen fiktive Wege aus diesen schrecklichen Lebenssituationen.

→ Beispiel: Charles Dickens, *Oliver Twist*

Ästhetizismus ***(Aestheticism)***

- Diese Bewegung am Ende des Jahrhunderts betrachtet Schönheit als den Sinn der Kunst: die Idee, soziale oder politische Themen durch Kunst auszudrücken, wurde abgelehnt.
- Autoren spielten gerne mit der Sprache: Metapher und Wortspiel wurden häufig verwendet.

→ Beispiel: Oscar Wilde, *The Picture of Dorian Grey*

USA

- 1830–1870 war die erste Hochphase der US-Literatur.
- Die eindrucksvollen Naturlandschaften des Kontinents wurden oft thematisiert: die literarische Bewegung heißt **Transzendentalismus**, Sie wurde von Autoren wie Thoreau und Emerson gegründet.
- Die Menschen sollten dazu bewegt werden, die Natur individuell und intuitiv zu erleben.

→ Beispiel: Henry David Thoreau, *Walden*

Das 20. Jahrhundert

NEUE RICHTUNGEN FÜR DIE LITERATUR

- **Moderne =** die Literatur vom Anfang des Jahrhunderts
- **Postmoderne =** die Zeit nach dem Zweiten Weltkrieg
- **Postkoloniale Literatur =** Autoren und Autorinnen aus ehemaligen britischen Kolonien schreiben über ihre Erlebnisse.

Die Moderne ***(Modernism/High Modernism)***

- Der Höhepunkt war die Zeit zwischen den beiden Weltkriegen.
- Die Innenwelt der Figuren steht im Mittelpunkt: Ihr Innenleben wird durch Bewusstseinsstrom *(stream of consciousness)* und inneren Monolog *(inner monologue)* dargestellt.
- Das Drama erlebt eine neue Blütezeit (z. B. Stücke von Arthur Miller).

→ Beispiele: Virginia Woolf, *Mrs Dalloway*;

Die Postmoderne *(Postmodernism)*

- In der Nachkriegszeit wurde mit experimentelle Erzählformen gespielt: Das Erzählen an sich ist oft ein Thema solcher Werken.
- Man setzt sich mit der Geschichte auseinander.
- Der inneren Zerfall der postmodernen Gesellschaft wird thematisiert.
- Postmoderne Autoren und Autorinnen stellen Konzepte wie Moralität, Menschlichkeit oder Wahrheit in Frage.

→ Beispiele: Doris Lessing, *The Golden Notebook*; Margaret Attwood, *The Handmaid's Tale*

Postkoloniale Literatur *(Postcolonial Literature)*

- Autoren und Autorinnen aus ehemals unterworfenen Kulturen schreiben über ihre Erlebnisse.
- Fragen der Identität werden bearbeitet.
- Großstadtleben, wenn man „anders" ist: Menschen, die wegen ihrer Abstammung, Klassenzugehörigkeit oder sexueller Orientierung ausgegrenzt werden.
- Ebenso schreiben in den USA z. B. afroamerikanische, asiatisch-amerikanische oder indianische Autoren und Autorinnen über historische, politische und kulturellen Themen, die für die Identität und das Erleben der jeweiligen Bevölkerungsgruppe relevant sind.

→ Beispiele: Salman Rushdie, *Midnight's Children*; Alice Walker, *The Color Purple*

LITERATURGESCHICHTE IM ÜBERBLICK — Checkliste

→ Warum wird William Shakespeare als der bedeutendste Dramatiker seiner Zeit betrachtet?
→ Was versteht man unter „*Restoration comedy*"?
→ Wie unterscheidet sich *Robinson Crusoe* von der höfischen Literatur des 17. Jahrhunderts?
→ Womit befassten sich Schauerromane?
→ Welche Thematik zeichnete die amerikanische Literatur des 19. Jahrhunderts aus?
→ Was sind die wichtigsten Aspekte der postkoloniale Literatur?

STICHWORTVERZEICHNIS

A

Abbildungstyp 12
allegorical tale 153
Anforderungsbereiche 7
anti-Islam sentiment 44
argumentative essay 130
Artikel 146
Ästhetizismus 155, 156

B

Beiseitesprechen 120
Beleuchtung 142
Bericht 130, 146
Bewusstseinsstrom 156
Bible Belt 65
Bildanalyse 138
Bildbeschreibung 136
Bildinterpretation 138
Black Panther Party 75
blank verse 121
Botenbericht 121
brain drain 88
Brexit 35, 49, 54, 56, 57
Brief 143
British Empire 46
British Overseas Territories 49
Bühnenanweisungen 122
Bühnenbild 118, 122

C

cartoon 139
cavalier poetry 153
Chiasmus 112
Church of England 36
Civil Rights Movement 74
class society 41
cloning 104
colonies 47, 48
comic relief 119
comic strip 140
comment 130, 149
Commonwealth of Nations 52
compound noun 30
conditional sentences 27
Congress 58
Conservative Party 33
creationism 66

D

Democratic Party 61
Democratic Unionist Party 33
designer baby 106
devolution 34
Dialog 120
discourse 126
dramatische Ironie 123

E

ecology 89
editorial 130
Electoral College 63
Ellipse 112
Enjambement 114
erlebte Rede 128
Erzählsituation 127
Essay 130
European Community (EC) 55
Exposition 120
expository essay 130

F

fallende Handlung 120
Filmanalyse 141
first conditional 27
flat character 118
free verse 121
future forms 25

future perfect progressive 26
future perfect simple 26
future progressive 25

G
Gedankenbericht 128
genetic engineering 102
gerund 29
Gestik 122
globalisation 83, 84, 87
global warming 89, 91, 92
going to future 25
Green Party 33, 61
gun crime 79

H
Handlung 118
Hauptaspekt 137
Haupttext 118
Höhepunkt 120
House of Commons 32
House of Lords 32
House of Representatives 58

I
immigration 42, 70, 73
imperialism 48
India 50, 51, 52
infinitive 30
innerer Monolog 128
intelligent guessing 13
intensive reading 13, 18
international peacekeeping 96
international trade 84
internet 97
interpretation 149
Inversion 112
Ironie 139

K
Kameraführung 142
Karikatur 139
Kolloquium 10
Kostüm 122
kreatives Schreiben 148
Kulisse 122
Kurzgeschichte 125
Kurzroman 125

L
Labour Party 33
Leitartikel 130
letter 143
lyrisches Ich 111

M
manifest destiny 69
Mauerschau 121
melting pot 72
Methodenkompetenz 12
Metrik 113
Mimik 122
modal verb 28
modernism 156
monarchy 36
Monolog 120
multicultural society 43

N
narrative point of view 127
National Assembly for Wales 34
National Health Service (NHS) 39
National Rifle Association (NRA) 78
Native Americans 77
Nebentext 118
newspaper article 146
Northern Ireland Assembly 34

P
Parallelismus 112
Parliament 32, 36
passive voice 26
past perfect progressive 24
past perfect simple 24

past progressive 22
phrasal verb 31
Plaid Cymru 33
plot 127
postcolonial literature 157
Postmodernism 157
Präsentationsprüfung 10
present participle 29
present perfect 24
present perfect simple 22
present progressive 21
Prüfungskompetenzen 6

R

Rachetragödie 119
rags to riches 68
Realismus 155
Reimarten 115
Reimschema 113
Republican Party 61, 62
Requisiten 122
restoration comedy 119, 153
revenge tragedy 119
Roman 124, 154
Romantik 154
round character 118

S

Sachtext 12, 129, 131
Scanning 13, 18
Schauerroman 124, 155
Schnitt 142
Schreibplanung 18
Scottish National Party 33
second conditional 28
Selbstgespräch 120
Senate 58
showing 128
simple past 22, 24
simple present 21
Sinn Féin 33
skimming 13, 18
slavery 74
special relationship 55
speech 129
Sprachmelodie 122
Sprachregister 108, 143, 144
steigende Handlung 120
Stilmittel lyrischer Texte 116
Stoff 118
story 126
stream of consciousness 156
Strophe 113

T

telling 128
Textaufbau 133
Textfunktion 133
Textgattung 12
Textsorte 131
third conditional 28
Ton 142
Tragödie 119

U

Übertreibung 139
United Nations (UN) 96
US Constitution 60

V

Vers 113
Versmaß 113
Vortrag 145

W

war on terrorism 81
welfare state 40
Worterschließungstechnik 13

Y

young adult (YA) novels 124

Z

Zäsur 114
zero conditional 27